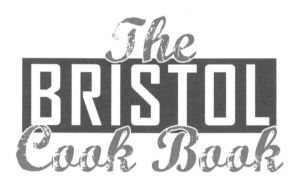

# The BRISTOL Cook Book

A celebration of the amazing food & drink on our doorstep.
Featuring over 45 stunning recipes.

**The Bristol Cook Book**

©2016 Meze Publishing. All rights reserved.

Second edition printed in 2016 in the UK.

**ISBN: 978-1-910863-14-5**

*Thank you to: Dean Edwards*

*Compiled by: Anna Tebble*

*Written by: Kate Eddison*

*Photography by:*
*Jed Alder (www.througheye.co.uk)*
*Paul Carroll (www.paulcarrollphoto.com)*
*Aaron Parsons (www.aaronparsons.co.uk)*

*Edited by: Rachel Heward, Phil Turner*

*Designed by: Matt Crowder, Paul Cocker,*
*Marc Barker*

*Printed by Bell and Bain Ltd, Glasgow*

*PR: Kerre Chen*

*Cover art: Luke Prest, www.lukeprest.com*

*Contributors: Faye Bailey, Sarah Koriba,*
*Bethan Littley, Holly Vincent*

Published by Meze Publishing Limited
Unit S8 & S9 Global Works
Penistone Road
Sheffield S6 3AE
Web: www.mezepublishing.co.uk
Tel: 0114 275 7709
Email: info@mezepublishing.co.uk

# FOREWORD

Bristol is a great city for food-lovers and is fast becoming a real foodie destination. It seems that there is always somewhere new to try when it comes to dining.

I was born and bred in Bristol and I am lucky to still live here with my daughter Indie.

Ever since I was a kid the Bristol food scene excited me, we have always enjoyed a fantastic mix of cultures in the city so it was nothing out of the unusual for me as a 10 year old lad to be tucking into Caribbean jerk chicken at the St Paul's Carnival as well as enjoying the fantastic bounty of cuisines and ingredients we are fortunate enough to have on our doorstep in Bristol and the South West.

Apart from my love for my home city, the dining scene is one of the things that has always kept me living in this wonderful, vibrant city. The pubs, cafés, bars, restaurants, street food vendors, delis and farm shops – they all provide such a diverse offering of places to enjoy the finest things our region has to offer.

What this book shows so fantastically is just how people all support each other here. It's great to see restaurants using local and seasonal produce that they have bought from a farm or supplier close to home. We are so lucky to have such amazing produce on our doorstep.

All these fantastic people and businesses have put our city firmly on the culinary map and I hope you enjoy taking a journey through the city's food and drink scene with this book. I am very proud to call myself Bristolian and any true Bristolian will tell you the recipes in this book are 'Gurt Lush' ha ha, enjoy.

*Dean Edwards*

# CONTENTS

# *Wine* UNCORKED

Corks of Cotham has been demystifying wines for the people of Bristol for the last 16 years, and with the Corks of North Street now offering the same independent advice and expert recommendations, there has never been a better time to try a bottle of something new.

Rachel Higgens and Dominic Harman had been living in London managing wine shops for a large wine retailer when they made the bold decision to up sticks and move to Bristol, the city that Dominic called home. They had an ambition to open their own independent shop where they could indulge in exploring some lesser known varieties and introduce people to some of the interesting options that are often overlooked in larger retailers.

When the first store, Corks of Cotham, opened in 2000, it became apparent that people were interested in trying niche products and learning about interesting grape varieties, and they responded by making their shop a place where wine is demystified, celebrated and loved.

They've kept the classics on the shelves, of course – classics become classics for a reason – but they have also put a lot of thought into stocking the shop with wines they want to share with Bristol. For Rachel, a fan of European wines, Italy remains one of her favourite places for good-quality and flavoursome whites and reds, but it's all about getting the best taste and offering good value for money for customers.

They have also got an enviable range of craft beers in stock, many from local breweries but with offerings from across the globe too. "People love to support local producers," explains Rachel, "and the beers from small independent producers can sell out as soon as we manage to get stock in."

She and Dominic love chatting to customers, whether they are looking to match a bottle of wine to a meal, see what they can buy based on their budget or sample some craft beers. Ask them what makes Corks of Cotham (and its sister shop, Corks of North Street, which opened two years ago) so appealing and they will both tell you it is their wonderful staff. They have five team members who are trained in all things wine and know the range inside out. With a team as committed to the business as they are, it's easy to see why they are going from strength to strength.

What does the future hold for Rachel and Dominic? The dream is to open a third shop which would also be home to a wine bar on the side… Bristol's wine lovers will be sure to raise a glass to that.

# Perfect PAIRINGS

The knowledgeable wine experts from both Corks of Cotham and Corks of North Street have provided some wine recommendations to go with all the delicious dishes in this book.

## AHH TOOTS
### Orange and Earl Grey cake
*Psychopomp Woden Gin & Tonic*

Longing for that slice of cake pick-me-up in the afternoon, but wondering what to drink with it? Well it's probably about time for a G&T, but not any old gin will do. As a true Bristol-native product, Psychopomp is the perfect gin for this cake – it has a gingery-citrus finish that harbours all the right flavours. Using small batch production from their distillery on St Michael's Hill, these guys certainly know what they're doing and, even though it's only available in Bristol, it's one of the best gins produced in this country. You can even visit them, sip a G&T and watch them distil.

## BAMBALAN
### Baharat lamb chops, roasted vegetable giant couscous, rocket, pomegranate and coriander
*Bodega Aniello, 006 Merlot*

Merlot has always paired well with somewhat spicier dishes, and the presence of the lamb in this medley of Middle Eastern earthy tones matches that even better. This Patagonian Merlot, chunky, a little perfumed, herbaceous and deeply earthy is what I had in mind. Grown on small plots that get picked at different stages, it creates the right mixture of fruit and spicy herb with almost a natural feel to it. Prunes, blackcurrant, mint and tarragon get swirled together in this South American wine, creating a generous background for the lamb chops to soak.

## BETTER FOOD
### Almond milk porridge with easy fermented fruits
*G. Miclo, Marc de Gewurztraminer*

A favourite breakfast addition of the French from Alsace, the Marc represents the morning kick that everyone needs. Usually served in coffee, but could also be had as a sipper, it spices up the creamy food, also bringing a touch of perfume to the table. Go on, you know you want to!

### Shiitake mushroom and roasted sweet potato risotto
*Scali, Sirkel Pinotage*

For a South African Pinotage this certainly is different! Elegant, perfumed, almost unrecognisable until those slightly rubbery smoky meats start to show through the fruit. Scali are growing these 20-year-old vines on the slopes of Paardeberg Mountain, Western Cape, and it shows. Great depth of fruit, summer berries alongside smoky plums and a bit of spice too. It complements the mushrooms and the roasted sweet potato just nicely!

### Salad selection
*Daumas Gassac, Rose Frizant*

Revered throughout France for their stylish yet traditional stance, the wines of Daumas Gassac have always had a good presence on our shelves. This superb Rose Frizant, obtained from young Cabernet Sauvignon vines, is perfect for the Salad Selection. Fresh and vibrant, but with enough fruit not to be austere, it fills the gaps between the leafy greens and the perky spices, mirroring most of the flavours with its summer berry and light citrus notes. Sunshine indeed!

## THE BOARDROOM

### Baked Camembert with garlic and wine, herbed butter and dipping bread

*Domaine de L'Espigouette, Côtes du Rhône Blanc*

Spreading like a fan around the Plan de Dieu and into the villages of Vacqueiras and Gigondas, Domaine de L'Espigouette is currently making some excellent wines, including their Villages White, a beautiful blend of Viognier and Grenache blanc. It is both fresh and creamy, releasing layer after layer of spicy summer white fruits, herbs and a mineral tone to keep things fresh. With every dip into the Camembert comes a sip, and with every sip the wine melts more into the aroma of the dish.

## BOSH

### Risotto bianco with tomatoes and basil

*Cantina Terlan, Terlaner Classico*

In the foothills of the Italian Alps lies the beautiful region of Alto Adige. Cantina Terlan is the finest producer in the region, some say in Italy, renowned for the purity and complexity of their wines together with unsurpassed ageing ability. This is an elegant example from them blending Chardonnay, Sauvignon and Pinot Blanc, pleasantly introducing early-ripening summer pears and nectarine fruit in a weighty but dry style. The long, tamed, but classy finish has some herb and mineral tones too. Just the salt you needed for those tomatoes!

## BRACE & BROWNS

### Frozen lemon parfait

*Akashi-Tai, Ginjo Yuzushu & Bertiol prosecco cocktail*

While this citrus fruit-infused sake might prove too tart to accompany the parfait solo, add this to sparkling prosecco and you have a fresh and dry yet fruity cocktail, great for this chilled citrus dessert. Make it up like you would a Kir and the salty-sour yuzu is tamed to perfection.

## BREW COFFEE COMPANY

### Smoked salmon with poached eggs, avocado, beetroot borani and za'atar on sourdough

*David Traeger, Maranoa, Verdelho*

From its Portuguese origins on the island of Madeira, Verdelho has found a second home in Australia where it is made into a dry style of wine. David Traeger is based in the Nagambie region of the state of Victoria and produces one of Australia's finest examples of Verdelho. Rich in tropical fruit with layers of melon, pineapple, peach and guava, it is a lovely match to the rich and diverse flavours of this dish.

## THE BRISTOLIAN

### Green tea pesto, kale and sticky tamarind chicken

*Susana Balbo, Signature White Blend*

This fresh and appetizing white blend of Torrontes, Semillion and Sauvignon Blanc has a beautiful mineral tone balanced by grapefruit and flowers to match the green tea. It has also spent some time in the barrel, so the chicken won't feel forgotten too. Susana Balbo is one of Argentina's greatest winemakers and has blazed a trail for female winemakers around the world.

## THE BURGER JOINT

### Pork, sage and apple burger

*Wild Beer Co, Ninkasi*

What happens when you make a saison beer, ram it full of hops, add some apple juice and then once brewed add some Champagne yeast for a 2nd fermentation process? The weird and wonderful Ninkasi. It's a beer like no other, with a creamy flavour and apple and citrus notes showing through. Great on its own but just as happy with pork or cheese dishes. The wonderful Wild Beer Co are based just down in Somerset and are producing a brilliant range of beers that are definitely outside of the box.

## BUXTON BUTCHERS

### The perfect steak

*Alain Brumont, Chateau Montus, 2010*

Also known as 'the Petrus of the South West (France)', its producer, Alain Brumont, is well known for making wine of great power and depth which rivals the great houses of Bordeaux. Tannat is the dominant grape variety in this wine, giving rich and concentrated notes of blackcurrant, plum, liquorice and slightly meaty undertones that are balanced by the chewy tannins that work perfectly with the marbling in the steak. It's a bit of a bruiser!

## THE CANTEEN

### Celeriac katsu curry with wild rice and pickled cucumber

*Mack's Frankenwein, Silvaner*

Proving there is more to Germany than Riesling, this Silvaner hails from the Franconia region of Eastern Germany. Grown in rich shell limestone soils that give the wine bags of minerality. With its almost spicy, citrusy apples and stone fruits, it will complement the fragrant side of the dish.

## THE CLIFTON SAUSAGE
### Trio of Old Spot pork; belly, cheek and sausage
*Bioca, Mencia*

Coming from the lesser-known region of Valdeorras, this little organic producer is currently releasing some excellent vintages of both reds and whites, focused on the terroir and local grape varieties. Bioca's Mencia is fresh yet has a lovely weight of fruit, sitting just right with the cheek or the sausage, and more so with the belly. It shows great structure, starting with mineral-infused red and dark fruits, tiny traces of aromatic cooking herbs and a bit of spice too. It is elegant, yet has enough body to not feel dim or drowned as it releases its broad and varied palate of flavours. It's great after dinner is finished too!

## DEAN EDWARDS
### Belly of pork with scrumpy and apple sauce
*Lopez de Heredia, Vina Gravonia*

As a white Rioja, the traditionalist-driven Gravonia from Lopez de Heredia is a perfect partner for pork. Rounded, juicy but full of complexity from its extra ageing in oak, it just fills the air with peach and creamy apples, custard, vanilla pods, wood spice and a dry lemon that keeps everything fresh. The finish is like a non-stop train to Eden town! The freshness from the lemon acidity really lifts this dish with the ripe fruit content rounding off the sauce. This is a Rioja like no other.

## THE FULL STOP CAFÉ
### Plum and red onion relish
*Domaine d'Escausses, Cuvee des Drilles*

A blend of Braucol, Gamay and Duras from the Gaillac region in South West France. Produced in a natural way allowing a vibrancy of fruit to radiate through, balancing the tang of the relish and enveloping the rich cheese if used in the sandwich. This deliciously refreshing wine can also be served chilled.

## GLASSBOAT
### Côte de boeuf, aligot, leaf salad and mustard vinaigrette
*Domaine la Soumade, Rasteau*

Nestled in the heart of Côtes du Rhône, in the village of Rasteau, Domaine la Soumade is producing several levels of wines from either the larger Côtes du Rhône Villages appellation or the distinctive, brambly Rasteau. This wine joins perfectly on the table with the côte de boeuf and aligot, with its creamy dark fruits, soft, but prevalent spice and with a matching cheesy-gamey aromatic pinch that sits just right with the flavours. Elegant yet full of rustic elements, this is Rasteau at its best.

## GRAIN BARGE
### Spicy seafood stew with sorrel oil
*Colomes, Torrontes*

From the oldest winery in Argentina, which also claims to own the world's highest vineyard. Located in the Upper Calchaquí Valley in Salta in the far north of Argentina, at this altitude the vineyard is subject to variations of up to twenty five degrees celsius between day and night – this helps the grapes retain huge flavours. Farmed biodynamically, it has fantastic aromas of grapefruit and citrus with hints of spice. On the palate, elegant with tropical notes and more spicy edges rounded and with unique character. The spice and citrus make this a perfect match with spicy seafood and the sorrel notes.

## INCREDIBLE EDIBLE BRISTOL
### Baked eggs with chard
*Arndorfer, Gruner Veltliner*

Eggs are notorious for being difficult pairings, but this Austrian natural Gruner is just the right thing! It provides the flavourful entourage for the creamy and aromatic eggs, shining through a muscular apple, quince and herb infusion. Partly fermented in big Slavonian oak barrels, it complements the dish with its creamy, almost spicy tone of macerated fruit and leaves your palate to wonder what comes next. It's fresh, it's creamy, it's the right one indeed.

## THE LAZY DOG
### Croquetas with bravas sauce and herb mayonnaise
*Suertes del Marques, 7 Fuentes*

This is a great introduction to the wines of Tenerife. It comes from a blend of several plots, all on volcanic soils, and its main component is the wildly aromatic Listán Negro, followed by a small amount of Tintilla. A juicy and refreshing wine that showcases the vivid aromas and flavours of the island and cuts through the croquetas and accompaniments beautifully.

## LIDO
### Seared Iberico secreto, fennel, peach, pine nut and basil salad
*Qupe, Bien Nacido Cuvee*

From the lesser known appellation of Santa Maria Valley in California, comes this excellent blend of Chardonnay and Viognier, produced by Qupe, a winery with a longstanding tradition for amazing whites and reds alike from this southern Californian outpost. Peach is the complementary flavour here, matching brilliantly with both the Iberico and the actual peach in the dish. Running alongside it are the oaky- vanilla notes that form a good partnership with those pine nuts in the salad. Fresh pineapple, curd and toasty elements appear every now and then giving the wine a fresh yet structured feel.

**Razor clams, chickpeas, jamon pata negra, amontillado, parsley and garlic**

*Casal de Paula, Blanco*

The North West of Spain is now providing us with some really interesting wines. This is a blend of Treixadura, Torrontes, Albarino and Godello resulting in a wine perfect for seafood. Delicious melon, apple and lemon fruits on the palate with a gorgeous freshness. The Atlantic influence gives the wine a soft salty edge which underlines its character.

## LITTLE KITCHEN COOKERY SCHOOL
### Mar hor
*Bischofliche Weinguter Trier, Riesling Off-Dry*

Feinherb, as the Germans like to call the off-dry, is a masterfully skilled blend of wine made from late picked grapes and dry, zesty young Riesling. This is the perfect wine for spicy food which needs a touch of sweetness to balance the spice and crisp citrus as a refreshing lift. Mineral and full of fresh apples and lemons, it merely pierces the world of sweet juicy fruits only to be tamed by the clean, crisp mineral notes that dominate it.

## THE MALL DELI
### Smoky aubergine and chickpea salad
*Johanneshof Reinisch Zweigelt*

The vineyards are just North of Vienna in Lower Austria, a region with a history of over two thousand years of wine-making. Zweigelt was named after the Austrian plant-breeder Prof. Fritz Zweigelt, who created this successful cross of Blaufränkisch and St. Laurent. Barrel-ageing for twelve months produces the wonderful flavours of plums, cherries and soft fine tannins. The depth and balance of acidity make this a great accompaniment for the smoky notes in the salad.

### Chocolate stout cake
*Wiper & True Milkshake*

From one of the best regarded Bristol breweries. A milk stout uses sugar made from cow's milk to give the beer a sweet, creamy tone. Bristol breweries were once famous for brewing the best milk stouts around. A take on the traditional recipe using copious amounts of chocolate malts and vanilla pods to create a rich, velvety and satisfying dark beer. Cake and beer heaven.

## MANNA
### Over-night lamb shoulder with slow-cooked cauliflower, roasted sweet peppers and salsa verde
*Cataldi Madonna: Malandrino, Montepulciano D'Abruzzo*

Serenading through a fruit concerto, this Montepulciano example rounds off the dish in such a brilliant way. Intense aromas of black cherry, plum, blueberries and violets, on a backbone of tannin that gives the wine elegance, too. Herbaceous and still fresh on the finish to match that lovely salsa verde. Hailing from the Abruzzo region in eastern Italy, Cataldi Madonna are leaders in their field, producing the best Montepulcianos and Pecorinos around.

## NO.1 HARBOURSIDE
### Handmade tagliatelle with fennel, homemade ricotta and a fresh herb crumb.
*Niepoort, Redoma Branco*

Dirk Niepoort is one of the world's greatest winemakers mixing the long traditions of the Douro with much innovation. This is just one of the excellent white wines he produces with great food-matching ability. It has savoury notes, fruit and spice and a mineral freshness that comes forward after every sip. This makes for a lovely balance with the creamy and fragrant sauce to the pasta. Grapefruit, green pear, lime zest, walnut, rounded off by a creamy spice. The finish is long and complex, bursting with lots of herb and stone fruit.

## THE OLD MARKET ASSEMBLY
### Chicken broth
*Argueso, Las Medallas, Manzanilla NV*

A traditional bodega, established in the early 19th century, Argueso produces a superb range of Manzanillas. Las Medallas is an excellent example of 5 year aged Manzanilla. It is a great food accompaniment, having a wide spectrum of flavours, from salty-earthy fruit and spices to a lemony undertone that gives it a continuous freshness. On the nose it is fresh, zippy, somewhat spicy as well, and it shows a bit of sundried fruit with a touch of lemon. On the palate, it brings forward all those earthy spices, sea salt, preserved lemons and a savoury touch that just feels right for food. The finish is zesty, quite fresh and leaves a salty, oxidized fruit note that just lingers.

## THE OLIVE WORKS
### Pecorino salad
*Mittnacht, Pinot Blanc*

Mittnacht produce beautifully pure wines to organic and biodynamic standards in the heart of Alsace. The weight of this Pinot Blanc holds nicely with the Pecorino. Delicious notes of nectarine, pineapple and citrus lead into a wonderful finish with a characterful dry and spicy edge. A great classic and one of our favourites with food.

## THE OX
### BBQ glazed ribs
*Massaya, Le Colombier*

A Southern French style blend from the Bekka Valley in Lebanon. Spicy, juicy, dark fruit abound with an earthy rustic edge to compliment the sticky, smoky meat. Massaya is a well-established estate doing a fantastic job of promoting quality Lebanese wines.

### Salted caramel and chocolate delice
*Wild Beer, Wildebeest*

Can't decide between coffee or booze with your dessert? Then just do both! This coffee, chocolate and vanilla stout is rich and bitter-sweet, working perfectly with any dark chocolate dessert.

## PATA NEGRA
### Croquetas de jamon
*Contini, Vernaccia di Oristano*

A very traditional wine produced within the boundaries of Oristano on the western coast of Sardinia. The Vernaccia wine is aged in oak and chestnut barrels for 10 years under flor. This gives the wine a complex texture with layers of almonds and walnuts. Think of an Amontillado with more tang that cuts through these rich croquetas perfectly.

## PINKMANS
### Cornbread with smoked salmon and avocado salsa
*Moor, Nor' Hop Pale Ale*

It seemed only right to pair this US classic dish of cornbread with a North American hopped beer from one of Bristol's favourite breweries the Moor Beer Co. This fresh pale ale packs in a citrus punch to balance the sweetness of the cornbread, while aromatic floral notes complement the rest of the dish. In a can, and not just for hipsters.

### Apple crumble cake with cinnamon ice cream
*Poderi Colla, Bonme, Vino aromatizzato*

Bonme is an artisanal Italian vermouth like no other. Produced by the family estate Poderi Colla to an old family recipe, with a base of Moscato wine, it is a gentle vermouth more akin to a dessert wine. Whilst the family recipe is a closely guarded secret, it does include wormwood in its herbal mix. This is the main component of absinthe and Bonme means absinthe in the local Piedmontese dialect. Packed with bitter-sweet dried apples, apricots, quince and honey with an orange peel twist that is surrounded deeply by spicy bitter herbs. This is the best accompaniment to an apple pudding we have ever tried.

## RIVERSTATION
### Beetroot gazpacho
*Pinceszet Tornai, Zenit*

Native across Hungary, the Zenit grape showcases a plethora of summery white fruit, blossoms with a cool minty edge too. This one is produced in Somlo, Western Hungary where the volcanic soil and daily temperature changes aid the production of fine white wines. Looking at a summery version of a classic Hungarian Borscht, this wine certainly makes a great match.

## ROSEMARINO
### Arancini 'melanzane parmigiana'
*Benanti, Etna Rosso*

With vineyards on all but the westerly slopes of Etna, Benanti are iconic producers of the region. Using native varieties that we don't see elsewhere, and with volcanic soils and a distinct micro climate, their wines are elegant and distinct. The Etna Rosso blends Nerello Mascalese with Nerello Cappuccio. It has ripe, crunchy red fruits with a herbaceous, mineral edge and velvety texture that is a wonderful match to the arancini.

## SALT CAFÉ
### Salted caramel brownies
*Quinta de Gaivosa, 20-year-old Tawny Port*

Those brownies are going to want to drink this too! It's mesmerizing how this 20-year-old wine can come at you with so much flavour. First there are dates, then dried and desiccated plums, followed by nuts and spices. None too forward, but all merging into one stunning elixir. All these lovely layers of flavour complement and tame the rich sweetness of the dish. It is produced by the enigmatic Alves de Sousa family from some of the oldest vineyard plots in the Douro.

## SOUKITCHEN
### Baharat roasted duck, mujaddara and pekmez
*Casal Figueira, Tinto Adiado*

From the native Castelao grape comes this beautifully vibrant wine. Full of fruit and spices with a chunky body that matches the slight richness of the dish. Being a full natural wine has its perks too, as the finish is perfectly savoury and the bramble fruit inbetween is tamed, but with a lovely aromatic presence. It is produced by the brilliant Marta Soares in the Lisboa region of Portugal. Here she produces wine, just two in fact, with immense respect to the land and the local vines resulting in a magical essence of the region.

## SOURCE FOOD HALL AND CAFÉ
### Pork loin with smoked pig cheek and clams
*Quinta dos Roques, Encruzado*

In the heart of northern Portugal lies the wine region of Dao. It is home to one of Portugal's top white varieties, Encruzado. It is a fascinating grape with the virtue of being able to maintain the perfect balance of sugar and acidity resulting in serious, rich and structured wines with extraordinary ageing ability. Made by the Lourenco family at Quinta dos Roques, this is a striking example with luscious spiced peaches, roasted pineapple and crisp lemon citrus. Think Burgundy but a lot more funky! The richness of the fruit holds well with the fatty pork and smoked cheek, with the citrus lifting the flavours of the clams.

## SPICER+COLE
### Raw beetroot slaw with seeds, raisins, herbs and a pomegranate dressing
*Gasper, Malvazija*

With an ancestry dating back to the beginning of wine, Malvasia is a grape with so many profiles. This particular Slovenian example shines with fresh peaches, rich zesty notes of citrus and a lovely soft texture on the palate. Never far from a true quenching ability, this aromatic wine will put lots of smiles on many faces. As the grape has a long ancestry, so too has Slovenian wine production. With a long history of producing pure, age-worthy whites, in recent times wineries such as Gasper have taken this in to the modern day with wines showing a true sense of place now reaching our shelves.

### Fig, rosemary and olive oil cake
*Domaine Pouderoux, Maury Rouge*

There are figgy notes in the wine too! Lots of them, dried, fresh, packed full of spices and forest berries, tantalizing the palate in a dance of sweet and almost savoury style that you wouldn't want to let go. This is Maury, a sweet fortified red wine from the Roussillon, Southern France. Think Port but slightly lighter and more elegant. With every sip there are more rewards, as the wine starts to burst with even sweeter, darker dried fruits and finishes in an elegant and fresh manner.

## THE SPOTTED COW
### Bath chaps, fried pig ears, mustard mash, crisp capers and apple purée
*Domaine de la Terre Rouge, Tete a Tete*

From the foothills of the Sierra Mountains in California this is a rhone-style blend of Mourvèdre, Syrah and Grenache. Great character with juicy ripe berries and soft tannins, tobacco, pepper and some anise. A great combination with meat and spices. The sunshine-kissed grapes have a great balance of freshness and acidity, which are a perfect pairing with the rich meatiness of this dish.

## THREE BROTHERS BURGERS
### Smokey bro burger
*Cedre Heritage, Malbec*

From the original home of Malbec, amazing colour of dark ruby red with hints of violet. Intense blackberry with full spicy notes. Big, rich and dry with a balancing acidity. Grown in a mixture of soils, with some clay and limestone and only twenty percent barrel-aged, the quality of the grapes shine through. The perfect wine for a meaty, smoky feast.

## TOBACCO FACTORY
### Pan-fried sea bass with fennel salad and dill caper olive oil
*Ferrando, Erbaluce di Caluso*

An ancient variety from the far north of Piedmont, Italy. Very versatile, making wines from bone dry to lusciously sweet, Ferrando has gone for the former creating a wine that is perfect for white fish. With layers of green apple, lemon citrus, melon and herbs complementing the anise notes of fennel and dill.

## URBAN STANDARD
### Sticky toffee sundae with salted caramel sauce and pecan brittle
*Chambers, Rutherglen Muscat*

This one is a must! Luscious and aromatic, full of dried red fruits, rose petals, toasted nuts and a fresh, balanced acidity. It creates a cocoon of flavours around the dessert and makes you ask for one more! Rutherglen Muscat is an Australian specialty from the state of Victoria. Chambers are a family run estate started in 1858 and one of the most fabled in Rutherglen.

# Irresistible cakes
## TOOT SWEET!

A small independent cakery in the heart of St Nicholas Market, Ahh Toots is the place where art and cakes come together for truly irresistible results...

By day, Ahh Toots is best-known as a busy little café dishing up the type of breakfasts that have people queuing up day after day – sizzling free-range bacon is served in soft baps while Boston-Style beans on toast is the preferred vegetarian start to the day. Fresh sausage rolls are piled up ready to be devoured, and there are plenty of vegan and gluten-free offerings, too.

However, you may be distracted before you get to the counter... the old Victorian cart laden with the most stunning cakes in the city has passers-by standing in awe. From indulgent banana bread dripping with salted caramel to intricate cakes that are works of art in decoration, it is clear that owner Tamarind is a firm believer in "eating with your eyes" before taking that first delicious bite.

Tamarind had always worked in kitchens. She grew up in a little bed and breakfast where her mum had her helping out with catering from the age of 12. Surrounded by a love of food and gifted with natural creativity, it is no surprise that she progressed towards baking, where she could indulge in dramatic designs and artistic creations.

A degree in Fine Art under her belt, Tamarind has successfully brought her joint passions together to create some truly stunning bespoke cakes. She has been involved in some impressive collaborations, and was recently involved with the Young British Foodie events at The Tate Britain.

One of the things Tamarind most enjoys is creating individual cakes for people, be it for a wedding, a party or an event. She loves developing flavour combinations and striving to create something new, exciting and original that will excite all the senses.

There is something a little bit magical about Ahh Toots, according to its many fans who visit the quirky venue in the hustle and bustle of the market. Perhaps it is because everything is made in the little shed, perhaps it's the commitment to ethical suppliers and local produce, perhaps it's those mouth-watering sausage rolls that have become renowned at their tea rooms... or perhaps it's simply being part of that whole vibrant market experience where food, creativity and community come together so seamlessly.

AHH TOOTS
Cakery and Biscuitie

# Ahh Toots
## ORANGE AND EARL GREY CAKE

For this cake, we follow a simple Tunisian recipe but dress it up in typical Toots fashion. This recipe is gluten-free and the cake could also be dairy-free if you don't use the butter icing.

Preparation time: 30 minutes plus cooling time | Cooking time: 1 hour 30 minutes | Serves 6-8.

## Ingredients

1 lemon

1 orange

800ml water

1 tbsp loose-leaf Earl Grey tea

6 eggs

220g sugar

250g ground almonds

1 tsp baking powder

A pinch of salt

**For the butter icing:**

250g softened butter

250 icing sugar

A drop of bergamot oil (optional)

**For the drizzle:**

300g icing sugar

A little Earl Grey tea

**To decorate:**

Dried rose petals (optional)

Finely chopped pistachios (optional)

## Method

Grease and line two 20cm round cake tins. Preheat the oven to 160°C.

Poach the lemon and orange in a pan, add the water and bring to a simmer. Add the loose-leaf Earl Grey tea and cook for 1 hour.

Drain, cool and blitz in a food processor then leave to one side.

Whisk the eggs and sugar until thick and white. Add in the blitzed fruit and whisk a little more.

Put the ground almonds in a separate bowl with the baking powder and salt. Fold the egg mix into the dry mix and split the mixture between the two prepared cake tins. Bake in the preheated oven for 25-30 minutes until they're evenly light brown on top and leave to cool in the tins.

### For the butter icing

Put the butter and icing sugar in a bowl and beat until light and fluffy (we add a drop of bergamot oil). Turn the cakes out of their tins and sandwich together with butter icing. Coat the outside with a layer of icing, too. Place in the fridge for 30 minutes to set whilst you make the drizzle.

### For the drizzle

Place the icing sugar into a bowl and add the Earl Grey tea a teaspoonful at a time until you have a fairly thick and smooth mixture. Add more icing sugar/tea to get to a slow dropping consistency and pour this on top of the cake. Start in the middle and push to the edges to let it drizzle down the side. Too wet and it'll run right off the cake, too firm and it won't go anywhere. We decorate this one with dried petals and a pistachio crumb but you can use anything you like really!

# Feel-good FOOD

Bright, fun décor, an open kitchen and a unique terrace offering unrivalled views across the city, Bambalan is the ultimate hot spot for all-day dining whatever the weather.

Bambalan, the latest venture from the Hyde & Co group, means "lazy bum" in Costa Rican slang. Take in the relaxed ethos and vibrant colours and the name immediately makes sense.

Founded in 2010, the Hyde & Co group was the brainchild of Nathan Lee, Jason Mead and Kevin Stokes, a group of old friends who joined forces to collaborate on creating a bar that would bring something a little bit different to Bristol's nightlife. The result was Hyde & Co; the city's original speakeasy bar, and now, six years later, Bambalan is the newest addition to the seven-venue strong family. Having seen their previous ventures within the Hyde & Co group grow quickly, the team knew they wanted to try something new and, as they have become renowned for doing, provide a refreshing change to the Bristol food and drink scene.

Situated within the Colston Tower, the ground floor bar and kitchen sits below about 1000 office workers, making it the ideal spot for people grabbing a pre-work coffee, a quick lunch or an evening drink with friends. The atmosphere matches the colourful interior – cheerful staff embody the relaxed ethos and nothing seems too much trouble for anyone. There

are people nursing a coffee with a newspaper and groups of friends enjoying lazy breakfasts, while others sit quietly on laptops and families enjoy the light and appetizing menu options that are inspired by sunny cuisines.

All dishes are bright, zesty and pack a punch in flavour, thanks to the wood-fired oven, charcoal robatta grill and rotisserie. The menu is inspired by warmer climes – think mezze, dips, flatbreads, grills, salads and tagines – the ingredients are sourced as locally as possible, and all the food is freshly prepared on the premises.

The team behind Bambalan have spent a lot of time getting the drinks list just right, which was vital for their all-day dining concept. The tea and coffee list is a step above the usual offerings, and for later in the day beers, ciders, wines, spirits, tonics, coolers and cocktails are all represented.

The terrace is the jewel in the crown here. Its views are unique in the city and it offers a space that is unmatched anywhere else in town. Sipping on a beer in the evening sun and you could almost forget you were in the middle of Bristol… well, if you didn't have that amazing view to remind you, that is!

Bambalan

# Bambalan

## BAHARAT LAMB CHOPS, ROASTED VEGETABLE GIANT COUSCOUS, ROCKET, POMEGRANATE AND CORIANDER

The lamb is best if allowed to marinate overnight, so ideally prepare the spice mix the day before you plan to serve this dish.

Preparation time: 30 minutes, plus overnight marinating | Cooking time: 1 hour | Serves 4.

## Ingredients

**For the baharat spice mix:**
4 tsp paprika
4 tsp ground black pepper
1 tsp ground coriander
1 tsp ground cloves
1 tsp ground cardamom
1 tsp ground cumin
1 tsp ground cinnamon
1 tsp ground ginger
½ tsp allspice
1 tsp ground dried chilli

**For the lamb:**
8 lamb chops
Olive oil, for coating
1 lemon, sliced

**For the couscous:**
1 courgette, diced into 1cm pieces
1 aubergine, diced into 1cm pieces
1 red pepper, diced into 1cm pieces
1 red onion, diced into 1cm pieces
1 fennel bulb, diced into 1cm pieces
125g couscous
125g vegetable bouillon
A pinch of turmeric
A small handful of rocket
A squeeze of lemon juice
Salt and pepper

**For the dressing:**
500ml pomegranate juice
½ tsp rosemary
½ tsp thyme
1 small clove roast garlic
½ tsp Cabernet Sauvignon vinegar
¼ tbsp honey
¼ tbsp Dijon mustard
125ml second press olive oil

**To serve:**
Chopped coriander
Pomegranate seeds

## Method

**For the Baharat spice mix**

Grind all the spice mix ingredients together.

**For the lamb**

Rub the lamb chops with a little oil and the baharat spice blend with some lemon slices. Cover and leave to marinate overnight in the fridge for the best flavour.

**For the couscous**

Preheat the oven to 200°C. Place the chopped vegetables into a roasting pan, drizzle over some olive oil, season with salt and pepper and roast until softened. (Once cooked, leave the oven on – you will need it for the lamb.) Meanwhile, add a little olive oil to a medium pan. Add the couscous and sweat off for about 7 minutes until slightly coloured. Add the vegetable bouillon and turmeric and bring to the boil. Once boiling, reduce the heat and simmer until the liquid is absorbed. Once the couscous is ready add the roasted vegetables, a handful of rocket and dress with some salt, lemon juice and a good quality olive oil.

**For the dressing**

Add the pomegranate juice, herbs and garlic to a pan and reduce until thickened and syrupy. Pass through a chinois into a sealable container and chill. Once chilled, add the vinegar, honey and mustard and blitz with a stick blender. Slowly pour the oil whilst blending, making sure it emulsifies and thickens. Season to taste.

**To serve**

Heat a pan with a little oil and place the lamb chops in, sealing them for 2 minutes on each side. Transfer to the hot oven for 4 minutes, then leave to rest for 2-3 minutes. Place the roasted vegetable couscous on the warm plates, place the lamb on top and finish with the pomegranate dressing around the outside and on the chops. Sprinkle some chopped coriander and pomegranate seeds over too.

# How to
# BUY BETTER

Organic. Local. Ethical. Better Food believe in good, honest produce, and at their shops and cafés, they are making it easier than ever for people to buy ethical goods from a wealth of local suppliers, artisans and producers.

Established by Phil Haughton in 1992 as an organic delivery service, Better Food has come a long way from its original St Werburghs warehouse. Phil has lived and breathed all things organic since the age of 14 when he became a member of The Soil Association, and now has vast experience spanning over 25 years in growing, retailing, wholesaling and delivering organic food.

The journey since then has been a tale of triumph – it has seen Better Food become a limited company in 1998, move to The Proving House and become a conventional retail outlet in 2003 and began selling fresh produce grown on a 24-acre site in Chew Magna, which is now managed in collaboration with The Community Farm.

Meanwhile, in 2006 the ground floor area of The Proving House expanded to fill the entire space with an increased range of groceries, fresh produce, health and beauty products, alcohol, gifts and household goods. The store also hosts a café where you can sit and eat delicious dishes or grab a lunch to take away.

When the second store opened in 2010, it was a whole new venture for Better Food. Based in Clifton, the food hall and deli has its own unique identity but retains the company's local, organic and ethical principles at its heart.

The aim is to provide access to organic food to as many people as possible, while building a better and fairer community around food. In recognition of all this hard work, in 2013 Phil was awarded a Bristol Walk of Fame Eco Hero plaque at Bristol Zoo Gardens for his contribution to city life.

With a third store now open at Wapping Wharf, including an organic café serving breakfast and lunch seven days a week, aswell as early evening sharing platters and alchohol. Better Food is continuing to spread the organic word around their beloved Bristol. For Phil Haughton it's an exciting step forward in Better Food's aim to make organic food more accessible, while supporting dozens of local farmers, artisans and suppliers.

# *Better Food*
# SHIITAKE MUSHROOM AND ROASTED SWEET POTATO RISOTTO

This dish can sometimes be found on our special boards at St Werburgh's or Wapping Wharf. Perfect for lunch or dinner and great with a cold glass of organic Chardonnay. Use organic ingredients wherever possible.

Preparation time: 15 minutes | Cooking time: 40 minutes | Serves 6.

## Ingredients

*600g sweet potato, peeled and finely diced*

*1½ litres good-quality organic chicken or vegetable stock, hot*

*1 onion, peeled and finely chopped*

*3 cloves garlic*

*3 sprigs fresh thyme, picked from stems*

*300g shiitake mushrooms*

*300g chestnut mushrooms*

*400g arborio rice*

*125ml white wine*

*100g dried porcini mushrooms, rehydrated with 100ml boiling water*

*1 tsp butter*

*150g grated Parmesan cheese*

*Extra virgin olive oil*

*Salt and freshly ground black pepper*

*Pumpkin seeds, toasted, to garnish*

*Rocket, to garnish*

## Method

Preheat the oven to 190°C. Toss the diced sweet potato with some olive oil, salt and black pepper and roast for 20 minutes, keeping an eye on the colour.

Meanwhile, bring the stock up to a gentle boil.

Gently fry the onion, garlic and thyme in a pan over a medium heat in some olive oil without them colouring for around 5 minutes. Add the shiitake and chestnut mushrooms and fry for a further 3 minutes. Increase the heat and add the rice. Give it a good stir and pour in the white wine and porcini mushrooms in their water. Give a good seasoning of salt and black pepper. Turn the heat down to a steady, simmer and add the first ladle of hot stock.

Gradually keep adding ladles of stock and stirring until the stock is absorbed. This process releases the starch in the rice and creates a beautiful silky texture. When the stock has been completely added and you have a creamy and oozing texture, take the risotto off the heat and add the butter, Parmesan and a final seasoning.

Serve with the roasted sweet potato, toasted pumpkin seeds and fresh rocket. Enjoy!

# Better Food

# ALMOND MILK PORRIDGE WITH EASY FERMENTED FRUITS

This is a favourite off our organic breakfast menu in our St Werburgh's and Wapping Wharf cafés. We serve it with fermented and fresh fruits and it is also vegan and gluten-free! We use organic ingredients wherever possible. We love fermenting as it brings extra health benefits to your food. This is a quick and easy method to make fermented fruits, but it needs to be made 24 hours before you want to serve it.

Preparation time: 10 minutes, plus 24 hours fermenting | Cooking time: 5 minutes | Serves 6.

## Ingredients

**For the fermented fruits:**

500g pineapple, peeled, cored and sliced

50g fresh ginger, peeled and sliced

50g unrefined cane sugar

500ml unpasturised kombucha

**For the almond milk porridge:**

160g rolled oats (we use gluten-free)

200g ground almonds

600ml organic almond milk, organic soya milk or water, plus extra if needed

Sugar, to taste (optional)

**To serve:**

Toasted almond flakes and fresh fruit

## Method

### For the fermented fruits

Place the sliced pineapple and ginger in a bowl. Sprinkle over the sugar and gently massage into the fruit for 2-3 minutes. Transfer the contents to a Kilner jar and cover the fruit with the Kombucha; make sure fruit is completely covered. Leave at room temperature for 24 hours then keep in the fridge. They are ready to eat after 24 hours but the longer you leave them the more they will develop.

### For the almond milk porridge

Place the oats, ground almonds and the milk in a large heavy-bottomed pan over a medium heat. Add a pinch of sugar and stir with a wooden spoon. Bring to a steady simmer for 4-5 minutes; the more you stir the creamier the porridge will get. You may have to add more almond milk to reach the consistency you like.

# Better Food
## SALAD SELECTION

These salads work well on their own or together. The sprouting bean and lentil salad is made every day on the deli at Whiteladies Road. It is fresh-tasting, cleansing and extraordinarily nutritious. The dip is also served from the deli at the Whiteladies Road branch of Better Food. Use organic ingredients if possible.

Preparation time: 45 minutes plus 30 minutes macerating | Cooking time: 1 hour | Serves 6.

## Ingredients

**For the rice and lentil salad:**

250g puy lentils

250g basmati or brown rice

Marigold vegetable bouillon (optional)

2 tbsp extra virgin olive oil

2 red onions, peeled, cut in half from root to tip, and then finely sliced

250g carrots, peeled and grated

150ml apple cider vinegar

Sea salt & ground black pepper

**For the roasted carrot, cumin and butterbean dip:**

400g carrots, peeled and cubed

2-3 tbsp freshly ground cumin

175g dried butterbeans, soaked overnight and then cooked (or a 400g tin organic butterbeans)

5 or 6 cloves garlic

3 or 4 oranges, juiced

2-3 tbsp light tahini

150ml extra virgin olive oil

Sea salt & ground black pepper

**For the sprouting bean and lentil salad:**

1 red onion, peeled and cut in half from root to tip, and then very finely sliced from root to tip

50ml apple cider vinegar

2 lemons, juiced

600g (3 packs) various sprouting pulses (try the mixed bean and lentil, purple radish and mung bean)

30g flat leaf parsley, roughly chopped

25g mint leaves, roughly chopped

15g coriander, roughly chopped

Sea salt & ground black pepper

## Method

### For the rice and lentil salad

Rinse and cook the lentils and the rice separately in the bouillon (if using) and leave to one side. Warm a heavy-bottomed frying pan on a moderate heat, add the oil and the onions and fry until the onions begin to brown and crisp, stirring so that they do not stick. Season with salt and pepper. When browned, add the carrots so that they lie on top of the onions and then add the apple cider vinegar. Cook for a few minutes so that some of the vinegar evaporates. Combine all the ingredients and check the seasoning. Serve warm or cold.

### For the roasted carrot, cumin and butterbean dip

Preheat the oven to 180°C. Place a baking tray in the oven to warm through. Toss the carrots in 100 ml of the olive oil with the cumin and season with salt and pepper. By roasting the carrots in the cumin you are intensifying the flavour, just try not to let it burn as it can then taste bitter. Turn the carrots onto the warmed tray and bake for 25-35 minutes or until soft. When cooked, put the carrots, butterbeans, garlic, orange juice and tahini in a food processor with a little more sea salt and black pepper, and blitz. You are seeking a consistency similar to hummus. If the dip seems a little too thick, start drizzling the remaining oil into the mix whilst blitzing it. You can even add a little cooled and boiled water to achieve the right consistency. Check the seasoning – it may well need more salt and pepper – and serve warm or cold.

### For the sprouting bean and lentil salad

Place the finely sliced red onion in a bowl and cover it with the vinegar and lemon juice, set aside and leave for about 30 minutes. Empty all the sprouts into a bowl and gently break them up so that they combine together. Chop all the herbs – individually – and add to the sprouts. Season. When the onion has 'macerated', ie turned a bright and beautiful shade of pink, it has been 'cooked' in the vinegar and lemon juice. Add this to the salad with the vinegar and lemon juice. Gently combine all the ingredients and check the seasoning, it will probably need a little more. Serve immediately whilst it is still cold.

# Step into the
# BOARDROOM

The Boardroom was formed in Bristol in 2015 to serve extensive wine, beer and cider selections alongside great West Country charcuterie and cheeses. As you may have guessed from the name, it's all served on wooden boards!

The Boardroom is the brainchild of husband and wife team Alex and Sandra Hazzard, who were seeking to create something that reflected all the things they love and wanted to see in a bar. Having lived on several continents over the years, Sandra and Alex had returned to England with a whole new outlook on a food service and drinks led bar.

There isn't a fully staffed kitchen here, it's more of a deli counter with honest food being prepared in front of customers, brought directly to the table and presented to a high standard. You can even eat sitting at the large wrap-around bar that dominates the ground floor.

Located in the old city of Bristol, The Boardroom is housed in a listed building that dates back to the 1800s as a public house, but has also been a wine vault and a billiard room. The stunning setting lends itself to the low lighting and relaxed atmosphere; it's no wonder it was voted one of the top five most romantic places in Bristol.

The Boardroom is also known as a haven away from the loud hustle and bustle of some city centre bars, bringing a more refined approach to dining and going out for professionals, couples and groups of friends.

Every week Alex and Sandra drive out to the Somerset countryside to visit the dairies in person, which allows them to vary and experiment with their cheese selection constantly in order to produce some of the best locally-inspired cheeseboards they could possibly make. The couple have also managed to source some of the tastiest and most succulent charcuterie and cured meats available in the UK.

The wine selection covers in excess of 40 wines, with a temperature-controlled wine wall kept fully stocked to cater for a wide variety of tastes, from modest to adventurous. The draft beers and ciders are predominantly local, with exceptions such as Budvar and Erdinger. They even have their very own Boardroom Lager.

Wine and cheese evenings happen on a regular basis, with a great event space on the first floor being used for most of these.

There are rumours of the occasional ghostly rattle at The Boardroom… Perhaps the resident ghost enjoys the boards as much as the guests!

# The Boardroom
# BAKED CAMEMBERT WITH GARLIC AND WINE, HERBED BUTTER AND DIPPING BREAD

This is served with the decadent addition of some herbed butter. You can make your own with by adding sea salt crystals to butter along with some basil pesto, then store at room temperature ready to add to the dish.

Preparation time: 5 minutes | Cooking time: 15 minutes | Serves 2.

## Ingredients

1 standard unpasteurised Camembert

1 garlic clove

A healthy splash of Sauvignon blanc (the more you add, the thinner the sauce)

Salt and pepper

Parbaked French sourdough baguette, to serve

Butter

Basil pesto

Sea Salt

## Method

Preheat the oven to 225°C. Remove the Camembert from its wrapper and trim off the rind from one face. Place the cheese into a suitable ovenproof dish (some soup bowls fit this perfectly).

Chop the garlic finely and press into the Camembert, then add a generous splash of Sauvignon blanc and season to taste.

Bake in the preheated oven for 10-14 minutes, or until the top has browned.

Meanwhile, bake the parbaked bread at the same time. Parbaked French sourdough baguettes take 10 minutes maximum.

To create the herbed butter mix in basil pesto to taste and then add a pinch of sea salt.

Cut the bread in two and serve with the cheese, making sure you use the bread to stir the cheese into a creamy sauce as it is served, to make sure it all emulsifies together. Drop a knob of the herbed butter in the cheese as you stir for a decadent addition. The herbed butter can also be spread directly onto the hot freshly baked bread.

### To drink

The Sauvignon blanc used will pair nicely with the dish, or why not try a decent craft beer

Bon appétit!

# Amuse your BOUCHE

Canapé parties, wedding catering, amazing cakes, private dining, supper clubs…
Bosh is feeding Bristol's appetite for deliciously different homemade food.

From the first conversation you have with Juliet Clarke, it's clear just how much she loves food. She started her own catering company, Bosh, having worked in the industry her whole life, and it's safe to say she is a foodie to the core.

Looking back, she pinpoints two six-month periods working on an organic farm in Northern Italy as her biggest inspiration. The family were passionate about ingredients and cooking, they welcomed her into their kitchen and were overwhelmed by her culinary talent for creating traditional Italian dishes – and those Italians know a thing or two when it comes to cooking! It filled her with confidence to launch her own business back in Bristol.

Originally from Cheltenham, she chose to move to Bristol as she adored the vibrancy and energy that permeates the city, and her food reflects this zest for life. There are no set menus for Juliet, who loves working with clients to develop ideas. "Canapé parties are one of my favourite things to do," she says, as she loves the creativity involved in the bite-sized morsels. However she also caters all sorts of events from weddings to private dinner parties.

The supper club gained a loyal following when she originally ran them from home, being lucky enough to have a dining room that could seat 24 people. Word-of-mouth recommendations and social media meant that her monthly supper club was nearly always fully booked.

During 2013, Bosh started supplying cakes to local cafés and in 2015 Juliet took a break from running her supper club to keep up with demand. "It was quite an unexpected turn of events," she explains, "I began to supply one café and all of a sudden I had requests pouring in for my cakes." Her salted caramel brownie is now renowned across the city – she has been told it's possibly the best brownie in Bristol!

Having outgrown her home kitchen, Juliet eventually found some premises from where she could bake her cakes and restart her supper club. Now based at the Elephant House, Bosh's monthly supper club is booking out as quickly as ever. Diners can expect menus based on Juliet's travels – from Italy to Mexico to Sri Lanka, she always returns from holiday with a suitcase full of special ingredients and a notebook full of ideas.

As Juliet puts it, her passion is making food that makes people smile, which she sums up simply: "Let us amuse your bouche."

Bosh
Amuse your bouche

# Bosh
# RISOTTO BIANCO
# WITH TOMATOES AND BASIL

I first made this when I was working on an organic farm in northern Italy. They loved my risottos so much I was told that I'm 'at one with the rice'. The highest praise imaginable from a very discerning Italian! The first time I made this tomato risotto they were rather skeptical as it's not a typical Italian dish, but once they tried it they were indeed wooed by it.

Preparation time: 10 minutes | Cooking time: 30 minutes | Serves 2.

## Ingredients

**For the tomatoes:**

3 ripe tomatoes, roughly chopped

1 clove of garlic, smashed

Small handful of basil leaves, roughly torn

100ml olive oil

Salt

**For the risotto:**

40g butter (20g cold)

A good glug of olive oil

1 medium onion, finely chopped

1 stick of celery, finely chopped

About 1 litre homemade chicken or vegetable stock

250g carnaroli rice

150ml white wine

30g Parmesan

## Method

Start by preparing the tomatoes. Put the roughly chopped tomatoes in a small saucepan with the smashed clove of garlic, a good pinch of salt and the torn basil leaves. Cover the tomatoes with the olive oil. Put the pan on a medium heat until any bubbles appear. When this happens take the pan off the heat and set aside.

To make the risotto, add 20g of the butter and a good glug of oil into a heavy-bottomed pan. Add the onion and celery. Cook gently, with the lid on until softened but not coloured, stirring occasionally.

Whilst the onion and celery are softening, heat the stock on the hob.

Turn up the pan containing the onion and celery to a high heat. Add the rice, stirring for around a minute to coat it with the mixture and get the pan very hot. This is the important bit… add the wine and stir vigorously until the wine evaporates and the starch starts to come out of the rice. This will ensure a creamy risotto. Keep the heat moderately high as carnaroli likes a high heat.

Start adding the stock a ladleful at a time, stirring continuously. Add more once the previous ladleful has been absorbed and stir continuously. Scrape along the sides and the bottom to ensure the release of the starch and prevent it from catching.

After 15 minutes test the rice; you want it to be fully cooked yet retaining bite. Continue adding stock and stirring until the rice has reached this stage. This should take around 20 minutes.

Once the rice is done, remove the pan from the heat. Add the Parmesan and the remaining 20g cold butter and vigorously beat until it becomes shiny. Check the seasoning, adding more if necessary. Leave to rest for 2 minutes before serving. Spoon into bowls and top with the tomatoes.

# Braced for BRUNCH

After recently becoming infamous as the home of Bristol's Bottomless Brunch, Brace & Browns is also often affectionally know as the BBC canteen by those who work in the neighbouring BBC offices, and as home of the 'Best Sunday Lunch in Bristol' by the Bristol Good Food Awards 2014. Whatever you know it as, Brace & Browns is one of Bristol's most exciting eateries.

David Brown is the man behind Brace & Browns. Brace, he explains, is actually his mother's maiden name, which, paired with his family name of Brown, is a lovely nod to his parents' influence in his life. He left the corporate world in 2010 with the ambition to open his own bar, and in April 2011 Brace & Browns burst onto the Bristol food scene.

The building has been home to fine dining restaurants throughout its 60 year history, but David's intentions were quite different. He wanted to offer the style of food he loved to eat, and for him, it was all about finger food, nibbles and sharing. Small plates weren't as common as they are now, so this concept offered something new and original.

Being in the heart of Clifton, Brace & Browns became a haven for everyone, from students to high-flying media executives, its expansive terrace is the perfect place to enjoy a lazy lunch or post-work drink. The cocktail menu is varied with a few house favourites, but can anything be more British than Pimm's on the terrace?

Food-wise, Brace & Browns has a lot to shout about. They were one of Ruby & White Butcher's first customers and have worked with their neighbours since opening to get the best local produce. If you ask about the meat on your plate, the staff can most likely tell you the farm where it was reared, so it is no surprise the food is all made completely from scratch.

With a Bristol Good Food Award already under their belt for Best Sunday Roast in 2014, 2015 saw the arrival of a new chef and more new ideas. Head chef Andy Myatt curated the bottomless brunch menu after David shared his inspiration from a trip to New York. It exploded on social media and the whole city was trying to get in on the action – rumour had it you could get a table at The Fat Duck sooner than you could get a table for brunch at Brace & Browns!

With press coverage across national and local media alike (and a new booking system that managed to crash the exchange phone lines on its opening day!) the bottomless brunch at Brace & Browns is without doubt the hottest seat in the city.

# Brace & Browns
## FROZEN LEMON PARFAIT

Light, zingy and refreshing, this frozen lemon parfait is ideal for making ahead of time.
It will need at least 4 hours in the freezer before serving.

Preparation time: 15 minutes, 25 minutes chilling and 4 hours freezing | Cooking time: 5 minutes | Serves 12.

## Ingredients

90ml water

3 lemons, zest and juice

270g caster sugar

5 egg whites

2 tsp baking powder

530ml double cream

Berries, to garnish

## Method

Line a terrine mould or a 13 x 23cm tray with a double layer of cling film and set aside.

In a small saucepan, bring the water, lemon zest and sugar to the boil on a medium heat until it reaches 112°C on a sugar thermometer (if you don't have one, simmer for about 4 minutes until it has reduced to a syrup).

Whisk the egg whites and baking powder together until they reach soft peaks. At this stage, slowly whisk in the sugar syrup, bit by bit, until it's all combined. Keep whisking for a further 5 minutes until the mix has cooled. Cover with cling film and leave in the fridge for about 25 minutes.

Whip the cream to soft peaks and fold through the chilled meringue. Then fold through the lemon juice. Transfer the mixture into the lined terrine mould and set in the freezer for a minimum of 4 hours. To serve, unmould, slice and garnish with berries.

# It's all in THE BREW

It started as a coffee shop, but today Brew's food is as highly celebrated as its pots of coffee... in fact, it's the perfect place to enjoy breakfast, brunch, lunch and, as the name suggests, an excellent brew to boot.

Launched in May 2014, Brew is the brainchild of Matt Atkins. Coffee-lover and fan of good-quality food, Matt was a veteran of the hospitality industry by the age of 29, having worked in bars, cafés and restaurants since he was 16 years-old. A manager from the age of 21, he had a huge amount of experience in the industry when he decided to take a career break and travel to Australia.

It was during his antipodean adventures that he was inspired to open his own business: "I spent some time in Melbourne and I was overwhelmed by the coffee scene. The cafés were not just selling run-of-the-mill coffee with the same-old menus time and time again, there were so many places all pushing the boundaries with their coffees and food."

When he arrived home full of inspiration, his parents were keen to help him establish a family business. He found the perfect premises in the hustle and bustle of Clifton. "There was a lovely outside space, which is unusual in the area, and I could see the potential to make the existing café into something a bit different."

Project Brew commenced. This wasn't going to be like any of the eateries nearby. It wasn't only the food that was going to be ethically and locally sourced – so was the upcycled furniture.

The huge counter (which grabs your eye immediately as it's crammed with colourful goodies) is made from recycled chipboard, and the lovely yellow chairs were painted by hand: "At one point I had 29 chairs in my two-bed flat!"

The understated décor allows the food to speak for itself. The counter is laden with pastries from 7am, quiches, frittatas, salads, sandwiches and cakes. Breakfast and brunch run all day and there are always a couple of hot lunch options too. Everything is locally sourced and made fresh each day. The antipodean feel is certainly at the heart of things, but there is also inspiration from The Middle East in the food.

"I started with coffee as my focus – and I hope we serve a brew that is a little different to the usual offerings. We change it seasonally and try to pass on our coffee knowledge to our customers. However, suddenly we became known for our food, especially our brunches, so we definitely pride ourselves on our food and drinks evenly."

Awarded a Bristol Good Food Award 2015 for Best Café Food, it is clear that letting the home-made food speak for itself was exactly the right approach for Brew – and now the whole of Bristol is shouting about it from the rooftops.

Brew
Coffee Co.

Brew
Coffee Co.
House Blend

House Blend

Roasted by Clifton Coffee

Cornish Brie, Cherry
Toms, Caramelised
Onion Marmelade
3.65

Granola
Flapjack 1.95

...ffee Roa...
...d Dairy, The Go...
...ouse, Buxton Butche...
...ditional allergen information, just as...

BREWS
FAMOUS
Beef Chilli
served w' crispy tortilla
chips, house-made guacamole,
yoghurt and topped w' North
Devon Cheddar ...
♥ 6.85

...UNCH      3.25
            4.75
...1 salad   5.95
...2 salads  6.95
...5 salads  5.95
...ant 5 salads

# Brew Coffee Company

## SMOKED SALMON WITH POACHED EGGS, AVOCADO, BEETROOT BORANI AND ZA'ATAR ON SOURDOUGH

You need really fresh eggs for the best poached eggs. Our eggs come from The Good Egg Company, who are a family run business in Hilperton, Wiltshire. For us they are second to none and deliver the freshest eggs all year round. Our sourdough is the St Martin from Hobbs House Bakery, which makes delightful breakfast bread, and we use organic Yeo Valley natural yoghurt. The beetroot borani is made with homemade labneh (strained yoghurt), which needs to be started a couple of days ahead. You will need some muslin or thin cloths and some string for tying.

Preparation time: 15 minutes plus 24-48 hours straining | Cooking time: 1 hour 30 minutes | Serves 1.

## Ingredients

White wine vinegar

2 free-range eggs

1 slice sourdough bread, halved

Za'atar, for sprinkling

Butter, for spreading

½ avocado

65g smoked salmon

Lemon, for squeezing

Dill, to garnish

Olive oil, to drizzle

Salt and pepper

### For the beetroot borani:

500g natural yoghurt

500g beetroot, peeled

8g za'atar

2 garlic cloves, finely diced

25ml red wine vinegar

60ml extra virgin olive oil

Salt and pepper

## Method

### For the beetroot borani

Start by making labneh. Place a sieve in a bowl, lay out a series of muslin sheets or thin cloths in the sieve so that they overlap the edge. Place the yoghurt into the centre and then bring the ends together to create a ball of yoghurt. Slightly twist the excess cloth and tie with string or an elastic band. Place in a fridge and over the next 24-48 hours (the longer the better) drain the excess liquid caught in the bowl and twist the cloth to keep pressure on the yogurt.

Preheat the oven to 180°C. Place the beetroots in a deep baking tray, add water to about 2½cm depth, season with salt and pepper, then cover with foil and cook for 1½ hours or until a knife will push easily into the centre of the beetroot.

Once the beetroots are cooled add them to a food processor along with 4 tablespoons of the prepared labneh, the garlic, za'atar, red wine vinegar and extra virgin olive oil. Blitz until all ingredients are blended in to a paste and season with salt and pepper to taste.

### To prepare the dish

Bring a deep pan of water to a simmer and add a couple of glugs of white wine vinegar. As the first bubbles rise to the surface, have the eggs ready to crack and drop slowly in. You need enough movement in the water to move the eggs around, but not too much as the eggs will break down as soon as they hit the water. Crack the eggs and slowly lower them as close as you can to the top of the water. If the eggs don't move around at first then either turn the heat up slightly or help them by pushing the top of the water around the pan with a big spoon.

Meanwhile pop the bread in the toaster. Grab a plate, sprinkle za'atar around it and then butter the toast to place on the plate.

Spread the beetroot borani generously on one half of toast. Spread the avocado on the other half. Place the smoked salmon on the toast and fold to a twirl with your fingers. Squeeze a wedge of lemon across and season well.

By now the eggs should be ready (3 minutes); they will be bobbing around the top of the surface rather than submerged in the water. Transfer to a seasoned plate using a slotted spoon to dry slightly. Season again. Place the eggs on top of the salmon. Garnish with a little smidge of borani, chopped dill and a good drizzle of oil.

# A ray of SUNSHINE

This characterful little bistro in Bristol's Montpelier was slowly, carefully and lovingly brought back to life in 2012, and The Bristolian emerged as one of the city's most stunning spots to relax and enjoy good-quality, local food from morning till night.

The Bristolian, with its charming stained glass windows, quirky corners and colourful exterior was a forgotten-about gem in Montpelier until three friends spotted its potential at an auction in February 2012. Before they knew it, the gavel went down and this little corner of Bristol was theirs.

Ollie, Anna and James spent the next 10 months regenerating the small-but-perfectly-formed café to its former glory. When the doors opened in December 2012, people fell in love with its charm immediately. A sunny spot in every sense of the word, light streams in through the large windows, filling the interior with a warmth and brightness that is echoed in the ambience of the place.

"We wanted to make The Bristolian a warm and happy space", explains Anna. There is colour everywhere you look, from the cobbled outdoor seating area dotted with plants to the cheerfully-decorated interior and the beautifully vibrant selection of unusual salads that greets you on the counter. "We wanted to create a home-from-home feeling, somewhere where people would feel at ease, welcome and relaxed."

They do things a little bit different at The Bristolian. When your order is taken, they will ask for your name, so that when your food is ready they can just give you a shout. From hearty breakfasts, light lunches, their famous salads and sharing tapas plates to their irresistible home-made cakes, the menu is as cosmopolitan and eclectic as the ambience.

They have a licence for alcohol which gives the evenings a different vibe to the day-time café. There is a laid-back bistro feel as the kitchen begins turning out substantial main courses with weekly changing specials. From British classics, such as fisherman's pie, to aromatic delights such as Thai-style thick noodles, the chefs take inspiration from all around the world, while keeping their suppliers decidedly local.

They are great friends with their local baker, who delivers the fresh bread each day. The coffee, too, is roasted just 5 minutes away and the free-range eggs come from a local farm, as does all their free-range meat. It's this balance between being utterly Bristolian while embracing cosmopolitan charm that makes this little café and bistro something truly special.

# The Bristolian
# GREEN TEA PESTO KALE AND STICKY TAMARIND CHICKEN

This flavour-packed dish is a vibrant mixture of tastes and textures. You may not need all of the pesto, but you can use it for another meal. The chicken can be marinated the night before.

Preparation time: 30 minutes, plus 1-24 hours marinating | Cooking time: 30 minutes | Serves 6.

## Ingredients

**For the chicken:**

4 tbsp tamarind paste
1 tsp Tabasco
1 tbsp sesame oil
2 tbsp Muscovado sugar
3 tbsp honey
A 5cm piece of ginger, finely chopped
3 cloves garlic, finely chopped
1 tbsp pomegranate molasses
12 chicken wings or drumsticks

**For the green tea pesto:**

25 gram (½ cup) organic dried green tea leaves
A bunch of coriander, leaves only
40g basil
A handful of mint
½ cup blended sesame oil
1 teaspoon pomegranate molasses
½ cup extra virgin olive oil
6 cloves garlic
A 5cm piece of ginger, peeled
2 tbsp fish sauce (omit if vegan or veggie)
2 limes, juice
1 red chilli
1 cup peanuts
1 cup pine nuts
Salt and pepper, to taste

**For the hot salad:**

1 cup sunflower seeds
1 cup pumpkin seeds
4 cloves garlic, finely sliced
200g paneer cheese, diced
1 tbsp soy sauce
1 tbsp chilli oil
750g bag of kale, finely chopped
750g spring greens, finely chopped
¼ cup toasted coconut flakes
Sesame oil, for frying

## Method

### For the chicken

Mix together all the marinade ingredients, add the chicken and coat all over. Cover and put in fridge for at least an hour, or overnight if possible.

To cook the chicken, preheat the oven to 180°C. Cook the chicken in the preheated oven for 25 minutes or until cooked through.

### For the green tea pesto

Pour hot water over the dried tea leaves, stir and leave until leaves are soft and bigger; approx. 10 minutes. Drain and squeeze out the remaining liquid and remove any tough bits.

Soak in cold water for at least an hour, then drain.

Place all the pesto ingredients except the nuts in a food processor and blend until you have a smooth paste. Add the nuts and blend for a short while so that the pesto is still crunchy. Add salt and pepper to taste.

### For the hot salad

Coat the seeds, garlic and paneer cheese with soy sauce and chilli oil and fry in a pan until the seeds have popped and the paneer is golden.

Fry the kale and spring greens in a little sesame oil, and put a lid over the pan and cook with 1 tbsp of water.

Mix the kale and spring greens with the pesto and divide between the plates. Sprinkle the seeds and paneer cheese mixture on top, sprinkle with toasted coconut flakes, place the chicken wings or drumsticks on top and serve.

# For the love of BURGERS

Known across the city as being 'probably the best burger in Bristol', The Burger Joint has also gained a national reputation for its unique combination of quality and value... not to mention almost infinite choice.

The Burger Joint has sky-rocketed to success since it opened in August 2009. It began life with just a couple of staff in small premises in Cotham Hill. Owner Dan Bekhradnia had completed his degree at The University of Bristol and had been working in the restaurant business, where he had noticed that gourmet burgers were often the most popular choice on the menu.

Dan wanted to devote a restaurant in Bristol to doing the best quality burgers at reasonable prices. The Burger Joint was born and it's fair to say he hasn't looked back since! The restaurant soon outgrew its premises and moved to a larger building on Whiteladies Road in September 2012.

What is it that sets Dan's burgers apart from the rest? The Burger Joint has been listed in the national press as one of the top ten burger restaurants in the UK after all. Dan explains their four key principles are excellence, value, choice and provenance, and they stick to these values very firmly.

Even when the second and third restaurants opened (North Street, Bedminster in May 2014 and Fishponds in February 2016) Dan and his team have put the suppliers and quality produce at the forefront of the business. Meat is sourced from Ruby & White Butchers, artisan bread from Proper Bread, grocery produce from Ashton Farms and Bath Wholesale Fruiterers, and craft beers from Bristol Beer Factory.

Everything is then prepared fresh on-site and cooked to order, which brings us on to their unique ordering system and mind-boggling array of choice…

A mathematician customer has actually calculated there are 78,912,800 combinations. This is thanks to the genius way each customer can design their ideal burger. Pick the bread (including gluten-free options), the patty (from beef, lamb and chicken to kangaroo, venison or wild boar, as well as two vegetarian options), toppings (we're talking bacon, pulled pork, chorizo, six types of cheese, hash browns, guacamole, fried egg, mushrooms…) a choice of 21 home-made sauces and ten sides.

Carnivore or veggie, huge appetite or small – simply tick your choices on the handy order form and wait for your dream burger to be freshly prepared. It's no wonder The Burger Joint has gained a reputation for excellence that has travelled much further than the city's borders.

The Burger Joint

KITCHEN

Burgertown

# The Burger Joint
# PORK, SAGE AND APPLE BURGER

This is a burger that we often have as a special, and it always proves very popular. In the spirit of The Burger Joint, you can serve this juicy pork patty with whatever toppings and sauces you fancy, however we recommend topping it with melted smoked Applewood cheddar and a dollop of apple sauce for the tastiest results.

Preparation time: 30 minutes plus 1 hour to chill | Cooking time: 8 minutes | Serves 10.

## Ingredients

**For the burgers:**

1½kg minced pork (try to use a decent local butcher)

1 egg yolk

1 tsp garlic granules

1 Bramley apple, peeled and grated

1 white onion, very finely chopped

⅓ bunch sage, very finely chopped

Salt and pepper

**To serve:**

10 burger buns of your choice

10 slices of smoked Applewood cheddar

Apple sauce

## Method

Place the minced pork into a mixing bowl. Add the egg yolk, garlic granules and some salt and pepper.

Dab some kitchen roll on top of the grated apple to remove any excess moisture, then add it to the mixing bowl.

The onion and sage should be chopped as finely as you can (pulsing in a blender is ideal for this) and then added to the mixture.

Now mix all the ingredients together for a couple of minutes. (The mixture may feel a bit soft and wet at this point, but it will harden up in the fridge.) Now begin shaping into burgers. If you can find a round lid about 7-10cm, shape the burgers in this. Leave the burgers in the fridge for at least an hour to set.

For best results, cook the burgers on a bbq (a griddle pan works well also). They can be fried or grilled, too, but they won't taste quite as good. The burgers will need around 4 minutes on each side.

Serve each burger in a burger bun of your choice with melted smoked Applewood cheddar and a dollop of apple sauce.

# *Specialists in* KNOWLEDGE

One of Bristol's most trusted and respected butchers, Buxton Butchers not only supply the finest steaks to the city's finest restaurants, they have also been sharing their unrivalled knowledge of all things meat with their shop's customers since 2009.

Nigel Buxton has butcher's blood running through his veins. Coming from a long line of butchers in Bristol, he can trace butchery in his family tree as far back as the 1890s. He started working in the business himself at the age of 12 and since that day, he can truly say he has worked in every aspect of the industry from slaughtering, cutting and processing to being Head of Meat at a top-end organic specialist meat farm and Commercial Director at a multi-million pound meat concern.

His meaty experience hasn't been restricted to British shores, though. He has also travelled across the globe learning about how meat is prepared in countries across Europe and as far as America, Canada and Argentina. This desire to beef-up his butchery knowledge is something that has stayed with him to this day, so he is always on the look-out for the best meat that money can buy and bringing new skills and practices to his business back home.

When he opened his shop in Winterbourne in 2009 his premise was clear from the outset. This was going to be the absolute very best quality meat on the market. He sources the best meat he can find – this means he aims to source from local farms where the quality is good enough, but sometimes from further afield, as the quality will always be paramount. It comes down to lots of factors, from breed and farming practices to the abattoir where the animal is slaughtered.

In 2010 he had to take on second premises due to such high demand from restaurants and hotels who were sourcing their meat from him. With more space at his disposal, Nigel was able to have a purpose-built cutting area and dry-aging fridge, as well as huge holding fridge and walk-in freezer. A new extension in 2015 has been really exciting for the team, with a state-of-the-art dry-ageing Himalayan salt ageing chamber.

He has become renowned for his steaks, which are on the menus at some of Bristol's most well-known restaurants – The Lido, The Ox, The Lazy Dog, Glassboat and The Spotted Cow, to name a few. One thing all these chefs agree on is that Nigel Buxton's unique Himalayan salt chamber sets his steaks a cut above the rest. Let's take a closer look…

GAS OIL

# Deliciously DRY-AGED

Nigel Buxton's dry-ageing Himalayan salt chamber has become renowned across the city – and Bristol's home cooks and top chefs alike are putting in their orders for Buxton Butchers' dry-aged steaks.

It's something that is used as a mark of quality on menus across the city and discussed in depth by Bristol's beef fanatics at dinner parties, Buxton Butchers' famous Himalayan salt chamber is producing some of the tastiest dry-aged steaks in the region.

Nigel has been dry-ageing meat for many years. The main aim of dry-ageing is to concentrate and saturate the natural flavour. During the process the juices are absorbed into the meat, making the finished product more tender. Only high grades of meat can be dry-aged as the process requires meat with an evenly distributed fat content; so he uses his experience to select meat with the perfect marbling. Temperature, time, airflow and humidity are all key points, so dry-ageing units have to be temperature controlled to within a few degrees.

The meat becomes tender during the first 21 days, and after that the flavour continues to be intensified through the evaporation of moisture. Dry-aged beef is at its best at around 28 days, although the time it is aged can vary between 21 and 40 days. Nigel ages meat to specific requests for customers – he has even aged a piece of beef for 100 days!

The Himalayan salt chamber was built thanks to a long-awaited extension at the end of 2015, inspired by one of Nigel's trips to the USA. He came across Himalayan salt, which has unique properties of being able to remove moisture from the air. It has long been used for its therapeutic properties, but has found a new role in dry-ageing meat. Its mineral-rich makeup not only removes moisture from the air, but also purifies it and removes bacteria, as well as intensifying the flavour in the aged meat.

He built the salt chamber himself, as nothing like it was available in the UK: it was a real labour of love to create the ideal set-up for his needs. Was it all worth it? "Absolutely! You can not only taste the difference in the meat, you can see it, too." And it seems that Bristol's top chefs agree, as do his valued shop customers.

Buxton Butchers

# *Traditional* SERVICE

It's not only the high-end restaurants who get to reap the benefits of Buxton Butchers' knowledge and experience, his local customers at the family-run shop are also singing his praises.

The small family butchers shop in Winterbourne village is the heart of the Buxton Butchers family. Various members of the Buxton clan can be found working behind the counter, chatting to customers who they know on first-name terms and advising about cuts, provenance and cooking techniques.

If there is something Nigel Buxton doesn't know about meat, it's probably not worth knowing. Although Buxton Butchers are famous for their dry-aged steaks – and rightly so! – they also supply a whole host of other products from their traditional shop. Dry-aged pork loins are one of their most popular products, and they fly off the counter along with their hand-made sausages and burgers and the freshly cooked hams.

In fact the product range speaks for itself – people can simply cast their eye over the selection and ask the helpful staff if they don't see what they are looking for. What sets Buxton Butchers apart is their absolute focus on quality. Nigel's main philosophy in his butchery is that he will only ever sell meat that he would eat himself – and when you have standards as high as Nigel Buxton, you know the meat he sells is going to be exceptional.

He puts quality above everything else: "If someone comes in asking for a sirloin steak, but we don't have one quite ready yet, I won't sell it to them. I will tell them what is best that week, as I only want to sell meat when it is at its very, very best."

It is this confidence in their product and their specialist knowledge that has enabled them to build up a reputation for trust. And it is a reputation that is spreading far and wide, from the village of Winterbourne, across the city of Bristol and even further afield.

They have built up close relationships with their customers and work with people to fill individual orders and requests, whether it's a steak to be aged for a set amount of time or a big BBQ order for the weekend. Everything about Buxton Butchers celebrates the old-fashioned nature of a traditional butchers shop – with the very best customer service you can expect – while embracing a modern outlook and always keeping quality at the heart of everything they do.

Buxton Butchers Tel: 01454 773213

TOMATOES £2.85 kilo
CARROTS £1.50 bunch
CAULI £1.25 each
CABBAGE £1.25 each
BROCCOLI £3.20 kilo
ONIONS 85p each
MUSHROOMS £3.60 kilo
SWEDE 70p kilo
POTATOES £2.50 kilo
SPROUTS £5.73 kilo
RHUBARB

# Buxton Butchers
## THE PERFECT STEAK

This is how a Buxton Butchers tomahawk steak is cooked to perfection by Freddy Bird, executive chef at Lido. Cooking over wood or charcoal will give the best flavour, so this is best cooked on your barbecue. Add some wood to the coals for a sweet, smoky flavour, and remember to cook over white embers rather than flames.

Preparation time: 15 minutes | 16 minutes, plus 16 minutes resting | Serves 1, or 2 to share.

## Ingredients

*1 well-marbled tomahawk steak*

*¼ block of unsalted butter (about 60g), softened*

*8 salted anchovies, finely chopped*

*1 sprig of rosemary, finely chopped*

*1 dessert spoon brined capers, roughly chopped*

*Maldon sea salt and black pepper*

## Method

Prepare your barbecue. Season the tomahawk steak with Maldon sea salt.

Mix the butter with the chopped anchovies, rosemary, capers and a few twists of black pepper. Make sure it is all mashed up and then set the butter aside.

Cook the steak to your liking over the white embers of your barbecue. I recommend this incredible piece of beef to be cooked medium rare, keeping as much of the fat in the beef as possible, as this is where all the delicious flavour is. It will take around 8 minutes on each side.

Allow the beef to rest for the same amount of time you have cooked it for – around 16 minutes – with the flavoured butter on top. The butter will melt into the steak and bring out all the amazing flavours.

Serve with some fries or a green salad, if you like.

# *A celebration of* SUSTAINABILITY

From the launch of The Canteen in 2008 to the opening of sister restaurants No.1 Harbourside and The Old Market Assembly, this Bristol-based restaurant family has always kept seasonal, ethical and sustainable ingredients at the heart of everything they do.

Since it opened, The Canteen, situated in the heart of Stokes Croft, has had good food, a great atmosphere and free live music at its core. Nestled in Hamilton House, it's no surprise that music is one of the defining elements of this community-focused venue. Surrounded by artist studios and performance spaces, The Canteen attracts a diverse crowd who enjoy the open-plan set-up and buzz of activity. Freelance workers sit side by side with families during the day and in the evening people of all ages and backgrounds enjoy the vibrant live music scene.

The globally inspired menu is affordable, local, seasonal and diverse with plenty of vegan, vegetarian and gluten-free options – in fact The Canteen was awarded Best Gluten-free and Best Supporters of Local Produce at the Bristol Good Food Awards.

When The Canteen's sister restaurant No.1 Harbourside launched in 2010, it embraced the same philosophies of good, clean and fair food – no nasties to be found in the ingredients and a fair price paid to producers. The menu offers so much choice with creative fish, meat, gluten-free, vegan and veggie dishes, for which the talented team of chefs give credit to the amazing local ingredients they have on their doorstep. And when the doorstep opens out onto the iconic waterfront, it's no surprise that the oyster bar is usually heaving with people indulging in freshly shucked oysters, washed down with their seaweed gin!

In 2015, the family expanded to welcome its third venue, The Old Market Assembly, a collaboration with The Wardrobe Theatre. Like its siblings, everything about this eatery has people and planet in mind. We're talking sustainable, seasonal, local and ethical ingredients used in dishes that cater for all tastes and diets, whether you're hungry for a local saddleback pork burger, vegan Vietnamese salad rolls or just want to explore the range of organic sourdough pizzas from the in-house bakery. All three restaurants are proud to hold three-star awards from the Sustainable Restaurant Association – the highest you can get.

The bakery is rapidly growing, and Sanjay's sourdough has gained a serious following across the city. However, The Old Market Assembly, like its sister venues, isn't just about the food... a melting pot of events, shows every day at The Wardrobe Theatre, collaborations and community fun, there are plug sockets aplenty for working on laptops, a sunny terrace, parties with lots of dancing on Friday and Saturday nights, book launches, fashion shows... you name it, The Old Market Assembly has probably hosted it!

# The Canteen

# CELERIAC KATSU CURRY WITH WILD RICE AND PICKLED CUCUMBER

An original vegan take on a Japanese classic, this dish from head chef Christabel Courtauld is typical of the weekly changing menu at Che Canteen. The pickle needs to be made at least 24 hours in advance.

Preparation time: 30 minutes, plus 1-3 days pickling | Cooking time: 30 minutes | Serves 8.

## Ingredients

**For the pickle:**

1 cucumber, thinly sliced

11g table salt

85ml rice vinegar

20g sugar

**For the curry sauce:**

50ml vegetable oil

2 onions, peeled and sliced

10 cloves garlic, peeled

4 carrots, peeled and sliced

15g curry powder

3g garam masala

30g plain flour

1200ml vegetable stock

30ml soy sauce

2 bay leaves

15g caster sugar

**For the celeriac:**

4 heads of celeriac, peeled

200ml unsweetened almond milk

20ml lemon juice

180g plain flour

10g cornflour

5g salt

A pinch of cayenne

500g panko breadcrumbs

Oil, for deep-frying

**To serve:**

Wild and basmati rice, cooked

Spring onion, sliced

## Method

### For the pickle

Wash the cucumber and thinly slice. In a bowl, sprinkle the cucumber with 10g of the table salt and leave to stand for 5 minutes. Rinse and drain. Combine the vinegar, sugar and remaining salt until completely dissolved then pour over the cucumber. Refrigerate in a sealed container for at least 24 hours (up to 3 days is better).

### For the curry sauce

Heat the vegetable oil in a pan. Sweat the onion and garlic for 2 minutes before adding the sliced carrots. Stir until the vegetables are soft and starting to caramelise. Add the curry powder and garam masala and cook for 2 minutes. Add the flour and cook for 1 minute more. Slowly pour in the vegetable stock, stirring as you go. Add the soy sauce and bay leaves and bring the sauce to the boil. Simmer until the sauce starts to thicken. Add the sugar then sieve.

### For the celeriac

Slice the celeriac into 1½cm rounds. To make the batter, mix together the almond milk and lemon juice and set aside. Combine the flour, cornflour, salt and cayenne in a bowl then whisk in the almond milk mixture until a batter is formed.

Heat the oil for deep-frying. Dip the celeriac slices into the batter and then into the panko breadcrumbs until fully coated. Deep fry the celeriac until the breadcrumbs are a deep golden brown and the celeriac is starting to soften but still has some bite. Season.

### To serve

Plate up some rice. Top with the crisp celeriac slices and pour over the katsu curry sauce. Garnish with chopped spring onions and pickled cucumber.

# No.1 Harbourside

## HANDMADE TAGLIATELLE WITH FENNEL, HOMEMADE RICOTTA AND A FRESH HERB CRUMB

Get yourself a pasta machine and teach yourself how to make pasta for your family and friends. Nothing compares – that's why we always have a handmade pasta dish on the menu at No.1. This is a delicious vegetarian recipe by our head chef Jonny Byles.

Preparation time: 1 hour, plus 3-4 hours resting pasta | Cooking time: 40 minutes | Serves 4.

## Ingredients

### For the ricotta (makes 250g):

2.3 litres whole milk

240g double cream

1 tbsp Maldon salt

100ml lemon juice

### For the pasta:

250g '00' pasta flour

200g egg yolks (approximately 20 yolks)

### For the fresh herb crumb:

3 tbsp unsalted butter

1 medium banana shallot, finely diced

50g dried breadcrumbs

Half a bunch of flat leaf parsley, finely sliced

### For the sauce:

3 large fennel bulbs

1 tbsp fennel seeds

A healthy splash of white wine

1 tbsp unsalted butter

1 lemon, juice

Fine sea salt and cracked white pepper

Olive oil, for frying and roasting

## Method

### For the ricotta

Line a colander with muslin. Bring the milk, cream and salt to a rolling boil, stirring constantly.

Reduce the heat to a simmer. Pour in the lemon juice and continue to stir until the milk curdles.

Pass the milk through the muslin and tie. Hang in the fridge until the moisture is removed.

### For the pasta

Sieve the flour into a large bowl with a well in the middle. Lightly beat the egg yolks then pour into the well. Work together using a fork until it begins to form a dough. Empty the mixture out onto a lightly floured surface and knead for 5-6 minutes until you have a dough that is consistent in texture. Lightly flour and wrap in cling film. Rest in the fridge for 3-4 hours.

Cut the dough in half and dust each piece with flour. Pass the dough through a pasta machine on its widest setting, gradually working through the gauges. Use extra flour to keep the pasta dry each time you pass it through the machine. On its final run, dust lightly with flour and cut into tagliatelle using the attachment provided with your machine. Once cut, immediately hang the pasta taking care to hang evenly (at No.1 we use a clothes airer!).

### For the fresh herb crumb

Heat the butter in a pan, add the shallot and cook for 5 minutes to soften, then add the breadcrumbs and stir. Add the parsley, cook for 2-3 minutes and empty onto kitchen paper to cool.

### For the sauce

Preheat the oven to 180°C. Carefully strip away the fennel fronds and chop roughly, finely slice the stalk, clean the bulbs in fresh water and slice any parts that are discoloured away from the base of the fennel and discard. Cut the fennel bulbs lengthways into quarters and toss with olive oil, fennel seeds and seasoning. Roast in the oven for 20 minutes or until tender and slice when cool.

Cook the pasta in a pan of salted water heated to a rolling boil for 4-8 minutes until al dente. While waiting for the pasta, cook the sliced fennel stalks in oil in a pan until soft. Add the wine and reduce for 3-4 minutes. Add the butter, stir and combine. Add the fennel bulbs, tossing with the stalks and sauce. Add the pasta to the fennel along with a little of the cooking water. Toss in the chopped fennel fronds and season to taste with lemon juice, salt and pepper. Crumble ricotta over the pasta to serve, with a dusting of the herb crumb.

# The Old Market Assembly
## CHICKEN BROTH

A rich and satisfying chicken broth with 'shmaltz' dumplings from executive chef Scott Hislop. The quality of the chicken is important; we use Stream Farm Organic chicken from Somerset and you will taste the difference. This recipe needs to be started the day before.

Preparation time: 45 minutes, plus cooling overnight and 1 hour chilling
Cooking time: 2 hours 15 minutes | Serves 4-10.

## Ingredients

**For the broth:**

1 large organic chicken (around 2½ kg)

2-3 medium white onions, peeled and diced

4 carrots (250g), peeled and diced

2 sticks of celery, trimmed and diced

3 cloves garlic, peeled and finely chopped

5 fresh bay leaves

A couple of sprigs of fresh thyme

Maldon sea salt, to taste

A pinch of cracked black pepper

100g fresh flat-leaf parsley

100g fresh dill

**For the 'schmaltz' balls:**

4 tbsp chicken fat (schmaltz)

3 large free-range eggs

1 tsp sea salt

½ tsp freshly ground black pepper

200g 'matzo' meal, pulsed

## Method

Put the chicken into a pot big enough to let it sit comfortably. (You can joint the chicken if you like, but it's not a necessity.) Top up with water until it's 7-8cm above the meat and gently bring to the boil. Turn the heat down and simmer for 45 minutes.

Add all the vegetables and herbs (but keep the dill and parsley for later), and season with salt and pepper. Simmer for a further 60 minutes.

Remove from the heat, carefully lift out the chicken and vegetables and strain the remaining liquid through a colander. Leave the liquid to cool overnight. This will result in a layer of chicken fat forming. This fat is called 'schmaltz' in Hebrew and is essential for the dumplings and also utilises another part of the chicken.

Pull the chicken meat from the bones but don't worry too much about aesthetics. Simply pulling the chicken apart gives a simple, rustic look to the finished dish. Keep the vegetables as they will be going back into the broth later.

### For the 'schmaltz' balls

Take 4 tablespoons of schmaltz (it should be fridge hard and resembling lard), mix in the eggs and add 50ml of the cold chicken broth. Then add the matzo meal (you could use crackers or breadcrumbs but the matzo gives lightness to the dumpling). Chill for 1 hour then make ping pong ball-size dumplings.

Return the chicken broth to the pan and bring back to the boil. When heated through, add the dumplings, chicken and vegetables, turn the heat back to a gentle simmer and leave for 30 minutes until the dumplings are soft and springy to touch.

To serve, put 4-5 dumplings in each bowl and add broth and chicken. Add the roughly chopped dill and parsley and season to taste. The broth can be served with our fresh sourdough from our in-house bakery, or the homemade pasta in the No.1 Harbourside recipe, our sister kitchen.

# Bristol's
# BEST BANGERS

The Clifton Sausage has been serving up sensational sausages for over 14 years, and the appetite for their simple approach to top-quality British food just keeps growing.

A mainstay of the booming Clifton dining scene, The Clifton Sausage has been one of the community's favourite food spots for well over a decade. Although this iconic corner of Bristol is home to an enticing array of independent eateries, all offering delicious fare from around the world, The Clifton Sausage stands out as one of the original independents – and it is still flying the flag for irresistible British grub.

Owned and run by husband and wife team Simon and Joy, the aim today remains the same as it was 14 years ago: simple British food done well. "We wanted to put the simplicity of good-quality food at the heart of our restaurant, and we thought that sausage and mash embodied everything that good British food stood for. So simple, yet with the best ingredients and cooked well, it is still the most tempting dish people long for."

Simon and Joy put quality at the centre of their menu and developed close relationships with meat suppliers and created hand-made sausages to tried-and-tested recipes – they have actually been working with one of their main suppliers for 12 years now.

Simon's background as a chef means he keeps the food at the heart of the business and he works closely with head chef Daniel on the menus. The 'Clifton' sausage is their biggest seller (Old Spot pork seasoned with cider and wholegrain mustard), but people also love the classic sausage, where nothing more than a little seasoning detracts from the pure flavour of Old Spot pork. There are plenty of more unusual offerings and seasonal specials – the reindeer and cranberry sausage was a hit at Christmas, especially as the meat had been specially imported from Sweden to make them!

Over 100,000 sausages are consumed at The Clifton Sausage each year, but it's not all about bangers. Pork dishes are undoubtedly popular, but there is also fresh fish, seasonal lamb and local game on offer. Homemade sausage rolls fly out of the kitchen, perfect served with a craft beer, real ale or cider. Saving space for pudding is a must... comfort food classics are plentiful, but Simon will never risk taking their famous sticky toffee pudding off the menu. According to regulars it's a strong contender for the best in Bristol.

Relaxed, comfortable and welcoming, the service and ambience at The Clifton Sausage seems to marry perfectly with the menu. Honest, fresh, local and seasonal... classic British food, simply cooked well.

# The Clifton Sausage
## TRIO OF OLD SPOT PORK: BELLY, CHEEK AND SAUSAGE

Choose best-quality, pure pork sausages from your local butcher. The confit pork cheeks and the slow roast belly both need long, slow cooking times. They can be cooked at the same time, but you will need to start this dish with plenty of time to let them cook to perfection.

Preparation time: 30 minutes plus 1-2 hours marinating | Cooking time: 3 hours 30 minutes plus 30 minutes resting and 1 hour cooling | Serves 6.

## Ingredients

**For the roast belly of Old Spot pork:**

1 onion

3 celery stalks

1 carrot

1 head of garlic

4 sprigs of fresh thyme

1½kg Old Spot pork belly with the skin scored

1 pint good cider

½ pint water

Salt

**For the confit pork cheeks:**

6 pork cheeks, trimmed

1 sprig of thyme

1 head of garlic, roughly chopped

500g duck fat

Coarse sea salt

**For the sausage and mash:**

6 Old Spot pork sausages

1½kg Maris Piper potatoes, peeled and cut into 2cm cubes

100g butter

100ml double cream

Salt and pepper

**For the apple purée:**

2 Bramley apples, peeled and chopped

150g golden caster sugar

½ pint good cider

## Method

### For the slow roast belly of Old Spot pork

Preheat oven to 225°C. Roughly chop all the vegetables and place in a deep roasting tray with the thyme. Add the cider and water. Put the pork on the top of the vegetables and rub the skin with 1 dessert spoon of salt. Roast for 40 minutes, then turn the oven down to 160°C for a further 2½ hours. Allow to rest for 30 minutes before carving. While the meat is resting, strain the juices into a pan and reduce by half, then season to taste to make the gravy.

### For the confit pork cheeks

Sprinkle the cheeks with sea salt, add the thyme and roughly chopped garlic. Allow to marinate for 1-2 hours. Wipe the salt off the cheeks and place in a deep saucepan. Cover with duck fat and bring to a slow simmer for 2½ hours. Allow to cool for 1 hour and drain.

### For the sausage and mash

Meanwhile, grill or pan-fry the sausages, as you prefer, until cooked. Boil the potatoes in a pan of salted boiling water for 20-25 minutes until tender. In a separate pan, heat the butter and cream until all the butter has melted. Drain the potatoes well, then return them to the pan and mash well, adding the cream and butter. Season to taste.

### For the apple purée

Peel, core and chop the apples. Place all the ingredients in a saucepan and simmer for 15 minutes on a low heat. Purée with a stick blender or liquidiser.

### To serve

Serve the sausage, mash, pork belly and pork cheeks with the gravy and apple purée.

# Dean Edwards
# BELLY OF PORK, WITH SCRUMPY AND APPLE SAUCE

Since making his way to the BBC Masterchef final in 2005, Dean Edwards has been one of Bristol's best-loved chefs. He was born and raised in the city and although his career over the last decade has seen him working in some of the country's finest kitchens (such as the Michelin-starred and critically acclaimed Midsummer House in Cambridge) and becoming one of the nation's favourite TV chefs, his beloved city of Bristol has remained his home. He loves cooking with West Country ingredients – a passion which is exemplified in this dish with locally reared pork, regional apples and cider, and a selection of fresh-from-the-farm veggies. It is one of his choice recipes for cooking at home.

Preparation time: 10 minutes | Cooking time: 4 hours, plus 20 minutes freezing | Serves 4.

## Ingredients

### For the pork:

1kg belly of pork

1 onion, roughly chopped

1 carrot, roughly chopped

2 sticks celery, roughly chopped

2 cloves garlic, chopped

1 tbsp fennel seeds

2 sprigs fresh thyme

500ml scrumpy/dry cider

500ml chicken stock

Olive oil and butter, for frying

Salt and pepper

### For the apple sauce:

3 Braeburn or Bramley apples, peeled and cored

1 tbsp lemon juice

2-3 tbsp sugar

1 stick cinnamon

1 tbsp fresh tarragon

Salt and pepper

### To serve:

Sage leaves

Butter, for frying

Mashed potatoes

Seasonal greens (optional)

## Method

### For the pork

Preheat the oven to 200°C. Remove the skin from the belly of pork then score it carefully with a Stanley knife. Season it and place it between two baking trays, then roast in the hot oven for around 40-50 minutes or until crispy.

Heat some olive oil in a pan large enough to hold the belly of pork, then add the onion, carrot, celery, garlic, fennel seeds and thyme. Fry over medium heat for around 5 minutes, then add the pork, cider and stock. Bring to a simmer, cover and cook gently for 2-3 hours until tender. Remove from the pan and set aside.

Strain the braising liquid into a bowl then place the liquid in the freezer for 20 minutes, until the fat has solidified on top. Remove the fat, then return the liquid to a pan and reduce it over a high heat until slightly thickened.

Cut the pork into four portions then fry in a hot pan with some butter or oil until coloured. Leave to rest for 10 minutes.

### For the apple sauce

Roughly chop the apples then place them in a pan with the sugar and cinnamon and gently cook down over low heat. This should take around 10-15 minutes; add a splash of water if required. Season and add the chopped tarragon and a squeeze of lemon juice.

### To serve

Fry some sage leaves in butter until crisp. Place the crispy crackling on top of each pork portion and serve with some mashed potatoes and fried sage leaves. Accompany the dish with the reduced sauce and apple sauce for diners to add to their plates. You could add some seasonal greens, too, if you like.

# Cooking amongst THE BOOKS

A marriage made in heaven for those whose love of literature is surpassed only by their love of food, The Full Stop Café serves up simple vegetarian fare within the wonderful Bookbarn International bookshop.

Quirky home-cooking is dished up with plenty of imagination at The Full Stop Café – home-made soups with deliciously different flavour combinations, speciality sandwiches that are grasped in one hand while a novel is cradled in the other, as well as hand-crafted pastries and fresh salads, which are put together using locally sourced and organic produce wherever they can. Nestling within the book-lined walls of the Bookbarn is the perfect spot for indulging in an irresistible cake.

# The Full Stop Café
# PLUM AND RED ONION RELISH

This recipe can be made with redcurrants instead of plums, if you prefer.

Preparation time: 20 minutes | Cooking time: 1 hour 30 minutes | Makes 1 large jar.

## Ingredients

**For the relish:**

4 medium red onions, sliced

1 small red chilli, deseeded and finely chopped

2 small red peppers, diced

1 tbsp olive oil

1½ tsp Chinese five-spice mix

4 cloves garlic, finely minced

A small piece of fresh ginger, peeled and finely minced

400g plums, stoned and sliced into fairly thin moons (or redcurrants)

½ tsp salt

280g light brown sugar

150ml red wine vinegar

**For the sandwich:**

2 fairly thin slices of good bread

Butter, for spreading

Cheese, thinly sliced (we use goat's cheese or Brie)

## Method

**For the relish**

Place the onions, chilli and peppers in a pan with the oil and five spice and sauté on quite a high heat for a few minutes until soft. Turn down the heat and add the garlic, ginger and plums and cook until soft. Add the salt and give it a good stir.

Add the vinegar and sugar and heat gently until all the sugar has completely dissolved. Once you're sure it's all dissolved turn up the heat and simmer, stirring frequently to avoid it catching on the pan, for 1-1½ hours or until the vinegar has disappeared and it is a soft jammy texture.

**For the sandwich**

Take the bread and spread a thin layer of butter evenly over the outside (you don't need any inside). Put thin slices of cheese on the unbuttered sides and dollop some of your relish in the middle. Heat a dry frying pan or skillet to medium, then place the sandwich in. Let it fry slowly for a good few minutes on each side, pressing down with a fish slice from time to time, so the cheese goes melty and oozy inside and the outside is nicely browned and crispy.

# Thirty years AFLOAT

One of the oldest independent restaurants in Bristol, Glassboat has been serving classic cuisine on the water for thirty years – and it remains one of the city's favourite spots for simple French food.

Floating in the harbour at the heart of Bristol, Glassboat has been a symbol of the city's great dining scene for three decades – celebrating its 30th anniversary in 2016. Its owner Arne Ringner, who is still heavily involved in the day-to-day running of the business, was actually an accidental restaurateur back then…

Having fallen in love with the boat in 1986, he never originally intended to create one of the city's best-loved restaurants on the site. However, as serendipity would have it, the licence for the boat was for an eatery, so (luckily for the people of Bristol) Arne decided to turn the boat into a restaurant and Glassboat has never looked back.

The focus is decidedly French – although it's not the pretentious refinement that can so often be associated with French cuisine. It is best described as hearty brasserie-style cooking where top-quality ingredients are transformed simply into timeless classics.

Executive chef Freddy Bird puts sourcing the best ingredients at the top of his list: "We buy our meat from Buxton Butchers and some local farms, and we always hand-pick the cuts. And although we always choose fresh, seasonal and local vegetables from the region, I also travel to France to get those special ingredients direct from the markets in Paris."

They are understandably famous for their steaks, which have been aged for a minimum of 35 days in Buxton Butchers' Himalayan salt chambers.

But there are so many incredible ingredients being cooked, it's hard not to shout about them all… Noir de Bigorre ham, mussels, rock oysters, hand-picked crab, fresh tuna, courgette flowers, snails, sole, sea trout – each ingredient is cooked or prepared to perfection by a team of chefs who manage to balance that critical pairing of style and substance with effortless skill. It's clear to see why Glassboat's kitchen is known for turning out many a famous chef over its thirty year history.

Sharing boards have become very popular with diners looking for a relaxed approach to dining – a couple of the popular choices have included spatchcocked roast chicken, dauphinoise potatoes, French beans and Armagnac gravy, and roast Pyrenean lamb leg, ratatouille and garlic potatoes.

And what French restaurant would be complete without a thoughtfully stocked wine cellar? It goes without saying that the Old World vintages are well represented on the wine list, with some highly celebrated offerings from Champagne, Bordeaux, Burgundy and the Rhône – perfect to accompany a steak while overlooking the Bristol waterside view.

# Glassboat

# CÔTE DE BOEUF, ALIGOT, LEAF SALAD AND MUSTARD VINAIGRETTE

For such a simple dish it is important to choose the very best ingredients. We hand-pick our beef from Buxton Butchers, choosing the very best cuts with the best marbling. The beef is dry-aged in a Himalayan salt chamber, which means the meat can be aged for longer than usual. The result has been some of the most tender and full-flavoured meat I have ever tried! Personally I always choose côte de boeuf. It might not be the most tender of cuts but it has the very best flavour. We even take time to choose the best walnuts. Perigord walnuts have a delicious creamy flavour and texture, without a hint of bitterness.

Preparation time: 20 minutes | Cooking time: 18-24 minutes, plus 20 minutes resting time | Serves 2.

## Ingredients

**For the côte de boeuf:**

1 bone-in rib steak, approx. 1.1kg

**For the salad:**

1 tsp Dijon mustard

1 tbsp good-quality red wine vinegar

½ tbsp walnut oil

2 tbsp olive oil

Romaine lettuce

A handful of Perigord walnuts

Salt and pepper

**For the aligot:**

500g Maris Piper potatoes, peeled

250g Tomme d'Auvergne cheese

Milk and cream, to taste

2 cloves garlic, crushed until smooth with a little salt in a pestle and mortar

Salt and white pepper

## Method

**For the côte de boeuf**

Cook the steak to your liking (rib is best cooked rare to medium rare), turning regularly and leave to rest for at least 20 minutes.

**For the salad**

In a salad bowl mix the mustard, vinegar and seasoning, then slowly whisk in the oil so that it emulsifies. Throw the leaves on top with a handful of the Perigord walnuts. Toss just before serving.

**For the aligot**

Boil the potatoes in a pan of salted boiling water until soft. Drain and let them steam dry. Pass through a potato ricer and then, over a low heat, add all the cheese and a little cream and milk. Keep adding until you achieve a thick purée. Continue to stir until all the cheese is melted then continue to beat it hard with a wooden spoon until stringy like fondue. Check the seasoning and lastly add the garlic.

**To serve**

Serve the aligot immediately with the rested beef and salad, giving the salad a toss in the dressing as you serve it. The punchy Dijon and walnut oil dressing is the perfect accompaniment to the rich aligot and fatty beef.

# A table with A VIEW

From the Hold Bar to the top deck, the Grain Barge is a venue with character like no other – and with panoramic windows, there is no table where diners can't enjoy the incredible view.

Moored just across the water from Brunel's SS Great Britain, the Grain Barge occupies a prime position in Bristol's historic harbour. The restful effect of the waterside setting creates relaxed vibes on deck – there is no better place to soak up the character of Bristol's beating heart. Duck down to the Hold Bar and the atmosphere is irresistibly lively thanks to the regular music, comedy and other events that occur in the characterful space.

The Hold Bar's beer snacks have built up quite a reputation – choose between sausage rolls with spicy ketchup, mixed bean Scotch egg with piccalilli or pork pie with onion chutney, although most people can't pick between them so choose a selection and share them!

The food's popularity is thanks to head chef Hollie Wheeler's commitment to first-class ingredients, which runs through the Grain Barge's main menu as well as the Hold Bar's snacks.

Organic, locally sourced and fair-trade ingredients are used wherever possible, and usually from Bristol-based suppliers. Fresh fish comes from the Cornish coast though – caught each morning and delivered to the kitchen the same day. The bread is baked on the premises for use in the daily sandwich menu and bread boards. Whether it's sourdough, focaccia, brioche or rye, it's always been made by hand in the Grain Barge kitchen. In fact, everything right down to the mayonnaise and spicy ketchup is home-made!

Seasonality is important and the menu changes on a fortnightly basis to reflect the produce available - Hollie loves being able to create exciting special dishes based on what delicious fresh produce is in season.

With dishes ranging from tuna steak with tapenade, tomato and soft boiled egg to pan fried sirloin steak with fries, grilled tomato and café de Paris butter - the daily menu offers a great choice.

Any food that has been lovingly cooked from scratch needs to be accompanied by a good beer or glass of wine, so it's no surprise that the team at the Grain Barge have put a lot of thought into their range of craft beers in both the main bar and the Hold Bar. Their special relationship with Bristol Beer Factory is evident, as they pop up in a few of the dishes as well as behind the bar – order the beef shin and Milk Stout pie and you are on to a winning combination of the region's best produce!

# Grain Barge

# SPICY SEAFOOD STEW WITH SORREL OIL

Grain Barge is the perfect setting to enjoy a seafood stew with its delightful harbourside views. This stew is packed with spices and herbs, making it extra delicious. For best results, make the sorrel oil at least a day in advance

Preparation time: 20 minutes, plus 24 hours to infuse the oil | Cooking time: 2 hours | Serves 4.

## Ingredients

**For the sorrel oil:**

65ml vegetable oil

150ml extra virgin olive oil

½ tsp caster sugar

1 tsp lemon juice

45g sorrel (can be replaced with spinach)

1 anchovy fillet (optional), diced

**For the crab stock:**

1½kg crab shells

1 fennel bulb, chopped

2 sprigs of tarragon

4 sprigs of parsley

2 shallots, peeled and quartered

2 cloves garlic, peeled

1 star anise

4 plum tomatoes, quartered

1 bay leaf

**For the seafood broth:**

2 shallots, peeled and diced

1 tsp garlic purée

½ red chilli, deseeded and finely diced

1 tsp smoked paprika

1 tsp harissa paste

125ml white wine

250ml freshly squeezed orange juice

1 litre crab stock (can be replaced with a good chicken stock)

4 plum tomatoes, quartered

1 red pepper, deseeded and diced

8 langoustines

15–20 small clams or mussels (depending on size)

2-3 squid, sliced into rings

1 tbsp chopped flat leaf parsley

½ lemon juice

Vegetable oil, for cooking

Salt, to taste

## Method

### For the sorrel oil

Blend the oils, sugar, lemon juice and sorrel until smooth. Stir through the anchovy, if using. Cover and leave at room temperature for at least 24 hours to infuse.

### For the crab stock

Place all of the ingredients into a large saucepan, cover with water and bring to the boil. Reduce to a simmer for 1 hour, skimming any surface residue. Pass through a muslin cloth or very fine sieve, discarding the shells. Return the liquid to a clean saucepan, place on medium to high heat and reduce the liquid to 1 litre in volume. Cool down and refrigerate or freeze for later use.

### For the seafood broth

Using a heavy-bottomed pan, fry the shallots on a medium heat with vegetable oil until softened. Add the garlic and chilli, stirring for 30 seconds. Add the smoked paprika and harissa for a further 30 seconds, stirring continuously. Pour in the white wine, and reduce to a paste. Add the orange juice, stock, tomatoes and pepper, bring to the boil then reduce to a simmer for 45 minutes. Season to taste, then keep on a low heat to one side if using immediately, although it can be refrigerated overnight which will allow the flavours to develop.

### To serve

Heat a saucepan and sauté the langoustines in vegetable oil on a medium heat for approximately 15 seconds on each side. Add the clams, pour over the stew base, place a lid on top and bring to a steady simmer for 1-2 minutes until the clams start to open. Stir through the squid, still simmering without the lid for a further 30 seconds. Take the pan off the heat, stir through chopped parsley, lemon juice and taste for seasoning. Serve with the sorrel oil.

# Speaking EASY

Step into 1920s New York at Bristol's best kept secret prohibition-style bar Hyde & Co or opt for decadence on a grander scale at its big sister The Milk Thistle – whichever venue you choose, cocktails with character are going to be the drink of the day

Hyde & Co, with its speakeasy feel and low-lit atmosphere was the first venue from the Hyde & Co group, and was inspired by a trip to New York City where owner Nathan fell in love with the relaxed vibes of its hidden prohibition-style speakeasy bars.

A small and intimate space, Hyde & Co only opened at weekends at first. However, it didn't take long for Bristol's newest secret bar to become not-so-secret. As its reputation spread, it soon expanded its opening hours as it gained a loyal following and a reputation as a favourite for those in the know. For the team, much of the success was down to getting fantastic bartenders involved: "They took our ideas to the next level and really made Hyde & Co something special." The innovative cocktails quickly became some of the best in Bristol, thanks to the home-made syrups, intriguing bitters, tinctures and other ingredients.

A year after Hyde & Co opened, with many regulars now cramming into the tiny bar, the team were looking for a new venture where they could offer something on a larger scale. They discovered a grand and historic merchants building that had been empty for years and couldn't ignore its potential. Lovingly brought back to life, this characterful venue is now home to The Milk Thistle, which comprises a cocktail bar, lounge and private function room over its four floors. Its restored original features and grand elegance make it an ideal place to celebrate with cocktails, spirits, spritzers, wine and beers.

Another team of highly skilled bartenders run the show here, and they certainly know their Martinez from their Manhattan – and will happily shake (or stir!) you up anything that isn't on the menu. Although quite distinct, Hyde & Co and The Milk Thistle are bound by their unique, innovative and creative approach to cocktails, as well as offering something a little bit different from the mainstream – a touch of style from a bygone era.

# Hyde & Co
## R(H)UM CONFERENCE

A sweet and rich twist on an Old Fashioned inspired by the Conference cocktail first available at Death & Co. NYC. It has been part of the Hyde & Co menu since opening and has remained popular throughout. We use a pre-bottled blend of 4 styles of r(h)um – pre bottled for ease of service, consistency and the time allowing the liquids to mellow and blend together. Serves 1.

## Ingredients

20ml British-style gold rum

20ml Spanish-style gold rum

20ml spiced rum

20ml French agricole rhum blanc

10ml rich Demerara syrup

2 dashes Conference bitters (½ Angostura bitters, ½ Bitter Truth spiced chocolate bitters)

## Method

Blend the four r(h)ums together or use a pre-bottled blend. Add the r(h)um blend, syrup and bitters to a mixing glass and stir to chill and dilute. Fine-strain the cocktail over a large chunk of ice into a rocks glass and garnish with a piece of orange zest.

# The Milk Thistle
## MILK THISTLE DAISY

A zingy, dry, aperitif-style drink perfect to kick start a night out. As with the Conference at Hyde & Co, this is a drink that has been a constant on the Milky menu since she opened her doors – it is almost part of the building now! Serves 1.

## Ingredients

25ml London dry gin

20ml house-made pear syrup

20ml fresh lemon juice

Sparkling wine, to top up

## Method

Add all the ingredients to a mixing tin and shake briefly to chill. Strain the cocktail into a chilled coupette and top with sparkling wine (use a sweeter style of sparkling wine; we use Pignoletto Cleto Chiarli brut).

# Bristol's Incredibly EDIBLE GARDENS

Fruits, vegetables and herbs are springing up in the most unlikely places around Bristol's urban centre thanks to the inspiring support of Incredible Edible Bristol, from allotments, parks and gardens to curb sides and even railway platforms!

Founded by Sara Venn in January 2014, Incredible Edible Bristol is a volunteer-led community project inspired by the Incredible Edible movement. Horticulturist Sara had seen successful urban edible projects sprouting up around the world and a twitter conversation with human rights and environment scholar Anna Grear led to a meeting being set for March that year – a vision for an edible Bristol as its aim.

The meeting was a triumph, as people from across the city came together to discuss how Bristol could become the UK's first edible city. This was to be a truly inclusive project – if you eat, you're in. Two years down the line and there are now 32 gardens across the city, including an urban food trail across the town centre.

The trail begins in an unlikely spot on platform 3 Temple Meads, where an apple tree and a blackcurrant bush – a nod to Bristol being the birthplace of Ribena – start the edible journey. The trail goes through the Temple Meads concourse, taking in familiar spots such as Thomas Chatterton's gardens and St Mary Redcliffe Parish Church along the way, ending with five beds in Millennium Square Urban Allotments.

Tomatoes, squashes, fennel, brassicas, kale, borage, globe artichokes, rhubarb, strawberries, blackcurrants, redcurrants, apples, nectarines, chives, sage… you name it, the people of Bristol are growing it. And when all that nutritious home-grown fruit and veg is ripe? It's free for people to take home and eat.

What inspired Sara to get this inspirational movement off the ground in Bristol? "I love the idea of taking an unloved piece of ground and turning it into something that is not only beautiful but also productive," she explains. "This is a project that is all about action. We don't like to have meetings, we just like to get on with things. We help people transform their communities and offer support to those who need a helping hand to get their edible patch started."

With the new addition of an education programme to help schools grow food in whatever space they have available to them, there should be lots more incredibly edible gardens springing to life across Bristol in the future!

# Incredible Edible Bristol
## BAKED EGGS WITH CHARD

This recipe has been supplied by Bristol-based food blogger With Mustard who is a keen member of the Incredible Edible Bristol project, which encourages people to take food production back into their own hands. For frustrated urban growers with little outdoor space, it's a great way to enjoy seasonal produce; picking ingredients during a lunch hour or on the commute to and from work to create a meal. Comforting, garlicky and creamy, baked eggs are perfect for a leisurely breakfast or a light lunch. For this recipe you will need a generous handful of chard; pick more than you might think.

Preparation time: 10 minutes | Cooking time: 15 minutes | Serves 4.

## Ingredients

200g chard

200ml crème fraîche

1½ tsp English mustard

1 fat garlic clove, crushed

25g Parmesan cheese, grated

4 eggs

Salt and black pepper

Butter, for greasing

## Method

Preheat the oven to 220°C (200°C fan). Wash the chard thoroughly and shred into ribbons. Wilt in a saucepan with a lid on, over a medium heat. This should take around 4-5 minutes. Set aside.

Put the crème fraîche, mustard, garlic and grated Parmesan cheese in a bowl and mix thoroughly.

Grease four ramekins with butter and place on a baking tray. Divide the wilted chard between them. Add 2 tablespoons of the crème fraîche mixture to each ramekin and then crack an egg on top of this. Season with salt and freshly ground pepper.

Place into the centre of the hot oven. Bake for 8-10 minutes or until the egg white looks cooked and golden bubbles appear at the edges (eggs that have been stored in the fridge may take longer). Cool for a minute or so before serving, as the contents will be piping hot.

# It's a dogs LIFE

This independent dog-loving community pub has all the trappings of a good old-fashioned British boozer, but with a modern menu where quality really does come first. Welcome to The Lazy Dog.

A collaboration between long-time best friends Mike Cranney and Joby Andrews, The Lazy Dog is the combination of everything that is important to them in a pub... excellent drinks, fine food and a place for everyone to unwind.

They started in the bar trade together when they graduated from university. Their careers have taken them in different directions over the years, before bringing them back together for this brand new project. They came together with the aim of bringing this Victorian gem to life and their combined years of experience in the hospitality industry are evident in every aspect of the space, from the gin palace-style tiles and cosy booths, to the refectory-style modern dining area and bright beer garden.

Both of them having a background in cocktail bars means that the drinks menu is completely varied and the service is slick but friendly, the ideal combination for a modern pub. In fact there is an option for every occasion; a great selection of craft beers and real ales is matched by a cracking wine list, and skilful bartenders shake up stunning cocktails to order.

"As neither of us have a background in cooking, we have made sure we have excellent chefs in our kitchen and given them the autonomy to create quality-led menus," explains Mike. Head chef Elisabeth Julienne arrived from El Coque Mario Sandoval, a two Michelin-star restaurant in Madrid, having also spent six weeks on 'Top Chef', a Spanish professional chef competition. She took over the role from Oliver Reichold, who was instrumental in setting the direction of the menu, before stepping back and introducing Elisabeth to the restaurant.

Both Oliver and Elisabeth have built up relationships with suppliers, such as Buxton Butchers and Huntsham Farm, to make sure they get the best local and seasonal ingredients available. Elisabeth draws on her Spanish experience to add some international twists to the classic cuisine on offer.

The lunch time menus and specials boards change daily as the team source the best local produce and cook it all from scratch – including spoils from Bristol's foragers, whose finds often make it onto the menu. The Sunday roasts have become renowned in the city, when they roast a couple of rib-eyes, some lovely lamb and the best part of a pig or two... with all the trimmings, of course.

The Lazy Dog

# *The Lazy Dog*
# ELISABETH'S CROQUETAS WITH BRAVAS SAUCE AND HERB MAYONNAISE

This recipe is not quick, but it is definitely worth the wait. This specific recipe comes from my grandmother, who taught my mother, who in turn showed me. There really is no shortcut to make the perfect croqueta Española. The croquetas need to be chilled for 24 hours before cooking them, so start this recipe the day before.

Preparation time: 1 hour 30 minutes, plus 24 hours chilling | Cooking time: 3 hours | Serves 6-8.

## Ingredients

**For the croquetas:**

2 carrots

1 white onion

2 shallots

1kg chicken leg

200g stoned dates

100ml white wine

200ml water

500g butter

500g plain flour, plus extra for coating

1.2 litres milk

6–8 eggs, beaten

Breadcrumbs or panko breadcrumbs

**For the bravas sauce:**

50ml olive oil

1 white onion

3 cloves of garlic

1-2 chillies (optional)

2 tins tomatoes

20g sugar

20g salt

**Herb mayonnaise:**

2 eggs

A pinch of salt

1 lemon, juice

10g chervil

10g coriander

10g flat leaf parsley

500ml sunflower oil

## Method

**For the croquetas**

Preheat the oven to 160°C. Peel the vegetables and chop into small thin slices. Place the chopped vegetables along with the chicken, dates, wine and water into an oven tray. Season with salt and pepper, cover with foil and cook in the oven for 2½ hours. Meanwhile, prepare the sauces… and have a nice glass of wine!

**For the bravas sauce**

Peel the vegetables and chop into tiny cubes (brunoise). Heat the olive oil over a medium heat and add the vegetables. Turn up the heat slightly and cook until the vegetables are golden (2-3 minutes). Reduce the heat and add the chopped tomatoes. Wait for 5 minutes whilst constantly turning with a wooden spoon and then add the sugar. I prefer dark sugar because it takes away the acidity of the tomatoes without making it too sweet. Turn down the heat to the minimum and keep stirring for approximately 40 minutes. Once the sauce is cooked, season to taste. You can blend it if you prefer a smooth texture or leave it as it is.

**For the mayonnaise**

Making real mayonnaise is a process of trial and error to get the right texture, and every chef has their own secret to achieve the perfect consistency… work on yours! Add both eggs, a pinch of salt, lemon juice and the herbs into a bowl. With a whisk make a constant beating movement whilst adding the sunflower oil very slowly until you achieve an emulsion with a creamy consistency.

**Back to the croquetas**

Discard the chicken skin and bones. With your fingers, shred the meat and the vegetables until both are mixed together. Heat a big saucepan over medium heat with the butter in cubes. When it has melted add the flour and stir until they have gelled together. Add the chicken and vegetable mix and do not stop stirring. Once these two masses are mixed together, add the milk slowly as the mix bonds together. Keep stirring as the mix boils and thickens; we need a texture that almost sticks to the spoon. Once this has happened, take off the heat and pour the mixture into an oven tray. Cover it with baking paper and leave in the fridge for a minimum of 24 hours.

Prepare one bowl with the beaten eggs, another bowl with plain flour and another bowl with breadcrumbs. Take the croquetas from the fridge. By now they should have really firmed up. Put a few drops of oil on the palm of your hands and create ping pong ball-sized spheres. Put each one first into the flour, then into the beaten egg and then into the breadcrumbs. Heat the oil for deep-frying and fry the croquetas until golden brown. Once cooked remove from the oil and place on kitchen paper to drain any excess oil. Serve with the sauces.

# Making a
# SPLASH

An outdoor swimming pool surrounded by an award-winning restaurant, Lido is one of Bristol's most iconic dining destinations.

There are not many people in Bristol who aren't familiar with the renowned restaurant situated in the old viewing gallery of the Clifton Pool. Lido has turned out countless chefs who have learnt their trade in the famous kitchen before sharing their skills with the rest of the city, and the restaurant has been celebrated in the national press by the likes of Jay Rayner, Kate Spicer and Charles Campion amongst others.

Situated in the stunningly refurbished Victorian lido – don't be fooled by the tranquil pool and spa, this is certainly a destination for hedonism over health – diners range from suited business men and women to spa-goers in dressing gowns, all united by the laid-back atmosphere and complete feeling of relaxation on offer.

It was famously saved from being turned into flats in 2008 by Arne Ringner, who saw potential in the derelict yet characterful building, and restored it to its former glory with plenty of modern touches adding to its charm. One of the oldest surviving lidos in the UK, it now cherishes its Grade two listing from The English Heritage and is held firmly in the hearts of many a Bristolian.

As executive chef Freddy Bird describes it, it is "a place for everyone, where people can simply sit back and enjoy being looked after by the friendly staff". Set menus, breakfast in the bar, poolside snacks and 'swim and dine' packages are available alongside the main menu, but it is the à la carte offerings where Lido really flaunts itself as a premium dining destination.

The wood-fired oven turns out such delights as scallops with sweet herb and garlic butter for starters and duck breast with Morello cherries, Anis del Mono, rainbow chard, almonds and crispy potatoes for main.

The regularly changing tapas menu is a winner with groups of diners looking to share a selection of dishes. From olives, patatas bravas and guindillas to houmous, Syrian lentils and steamed mussels with charmoula, the dishes are inspired by flavours from across the Mediterranean and Middle East.

Since the building opened its doors in 1849, this has been a place for relaxation… and whether it's drinking, dining or a leisurely dunk, Lido continues to welcome people through its doors for a little indulgence.

# *Lido*
# SEARED IBERICO SECRETO, FENNEL, PEACH, PINE NUT AND BASIL SALAD

Freddy spends as much time sourcing his ingredients as he does cooking them. The importance of sourcing the very best ingredients is the only way to ensure the very best results! Iberico pork is to pork what wagyu is to beef. It has the most incredible marbling and incomparable flavour. Hunt down your local Spanish deli or buy online!

Preparation time: 30 minutes | Cooking time: 6 minutes, plus resting | Serves 4.

## Ingredients

2 heads of fennel

4 perfectly ripe peaches

2 handfuls of basil leaves

A couple of large handfuls of pine nuts, toasted

1kg Iberico secreto

A good splash of moscatel vinegar

A small glug of extra virgin olive oil

Maldon sea salt and pepper

## Method

Split the fennel in two and remove the core. Slice 1-2mm thick lengthways on a mandoline and set aside. Slice the peaches into wedges and add to the fennel. Add the basil leaves and pine nuts.

Season the pork liberally with Maldon salt then cook for about 3 minutes on each side. You don't want to overcook the meat as the all-important fat will be totally rendered out and you'll lose that incredible tenderness. Allow the pork to rest.

While it's resting finish the salad. Sprinkle over a good amount of the deliciously sweet moscatel vinegar (no other vinegar will do!), lightly season and add a splash of extra virgin olive oil. Gently toss together and serve alongside the sliced Iberico secreto. Eat immediately.

# Lido

# RAZOR CLAMS, CHICKPEAS, JAMON PATA NEGRA, AMONTILLADO, PARSLEY AND GARLIC

A true example of how a few great ingredients can make a ridiculously easy starter or light meal. There are so many varieties of clams, from your standard palourde or surf clam to tellines, razors and many more. They all work with this recipe. Cured Iberico pork fat (tocino) is available from some Spanish delis. Failing this you should easily be able to buy lardo from a good Italian deli.

Preparation time: 20 minutes | Cooking time: 5-10 minutes | Serves 4.

## Ingredients

100g cured Iberico pork fat or lardo

1 sprig of rosemary, finely chopped

1 garlic clove, crushed, plus 2 dessertspoons of finely chopped garlic

100ml amontillado sherry

1kg razor clams, washed

100g canned chickpeas, drained

A handful of jamon pata negra (or other cured ham), finely diced

A handful of parsley, finely chopped

Extra virgin olive oil, for cooking

Sourdough bread, to serve

## Method

Blitz the pork fat, rosemary and crushed garlic in a food processor until smooth. Set aside.

Next choose a pan large enough that it won't be too crowded when you put the clams in. Cover the bottom with extra virgin olive oil and add the finely chopped garlic. Fry until just cooked (do not let the edges start to brown!) then add the amontillado and boil off the alcohol over a high heat.

Add the clams, pork fat mixture and chickpeas and cook (with a lid on) until the clams just start to open. Gently shake the pan so that all the clams pop open without them overcooking.

Finally add the jamon and finely chopped parsley. Serve immediately in a large dish and pop in the middle of the table to share. Serve with plenty of sourdough bread to mop up all the juices!

# Lido
# SOURDOUGH

Baking requires a methodical approach with exact quantities and cooking temperatures. However, bread is far more about understanding your dough. When you make bread, treat the recipe as more of a guideline. We cook our bread in a wood oven, hardly the most precise piece of kit to work with, and I add more flour or water or work the dough according to what it looks or feels like. The more you bake, the more you'll understand it and the better your bread will become. Working with sourdough makes life a little more complicated as your active ingredient isn't as consistent as shop-bought yeast. If your starter looks a little tired, you'll need to perk her up with a little more flour and whisk in a bit of life. But very soon you'll get the feel for it and then you'll never want to buy a shop-bought loaf again.

Preparation time: At least 6 days | Cooking time: 30 minutes | Makes 1 loaf.

## Ingredients

**For the starter:**

Strong white bread flour (Lido use Shipton Mill #4)

Water

**For the sponge:**

800g starter

800g strong white bread flour

**For the dough:**

800g strong white bread flour

30g good-quality salt

500ml–1 litre water

## Method

**For the starter**

You can buy sourdough starters online but the process is incredibly simple. Just mix equal quantities of organic strong white bread flour with water and have a little patience. Some people mash grapes or apple in to theirs but there is enough wild yeast in the flour and in the air to do the job.

Feed the starter daily with equal parts water and flour. By day 5 you should notice little bubbles starting to appear. Within a few more days you should have a frothy and slightly sour-smelling mix; the starter is now ready to use. Timings can vary, but a simple rule is to keep the starter in a relatively cool place (not too close to a radiator rather than actually in the fridge).

**For the sponge**

First you need to make a 'sponge'. Mix 800g of the starter and 800g flour in a food mixer. It won't be thick enough to knead but it will eventually mix to a thick milkshake consistency. Leave overnight (or 6 hours). It should have doubled in size and be foamy.

**For the dough**

Add 800g strong white bread flour and 30g salt to the sponge. Knead it with the dough hook on low speed. You want a thick dough that works out the lumps and starts to stretch and not tear too easily; you may need to add more flour. Now slacken it off with water – start with 500ml (but it could need up to a litre). It should have a glossy sheen, not tear easily and run out of your hands a little too easily.

Flour a bread basket, just enough to prevent the dough from sticking. Leave the loaf to prove for several hours (until it has risen to the top of your basket or will rise no further).

Freddy bakes his sourdough in a wood oven and can tip the dough directly on to the stone base. The heat of the oven and the wet dough also helps to create a great crust. To replicate this at home, preheat the oven to 250°C with a pizza stone in and an empty roasting tray in the bottom.

Tip the loaf on to the hot pizza stone and, just before closing the oven, add about 100ml water into the tray in the bottom of the oven and quickly close the door. After 15 minutes drop the temperature to 220°C and leave for 15 minutes. To test if the loaf is cooked, hold it in one hand using a tea towel and tap the bottom. You want it to sound hollow. Leave to cool on a rack before eating.

# Cooking up CONFIDENCE

Little Kitchen Cookery School is the ideal place for anyone who wants to add something new to their culinary repertoire... or simply have a great day out and make some friends along the way.

Claire and Madeleine cooked up their dream business idea at the beginning of 2014, a couple of years after they first met. Claire was running a street food business and Madeleine was a food and cookery teacher, and they both had a spirited passion for everything related to food, so between them they had the perfect experience to offer cooking lessons, workshops and courses.

By June 2014, Little Kitchen opened its doors to reveal a light, bright, well-equipped and utterly welcoming cookery school. Their premise was to get ordinary people cooking simple dishes from scratch, to make it into an enjoyable and social affair that was as much an evening out as it was a learning experience.

Some of the favourite classes involve people coming along with a bottle of wine, so that once they have cooked a dish, everyone in the class sits down together and enjoys the fruits of their labour washed down with a glass of vino and plenty of laughter.

There are also some more technical classes on offer – the macaron-making and bread-making are really popular. Madeleine is the baking queen and tends to run these courses,

along with one of their fabulous tutors Louise who is a whiz with all things chocolate and patisserie. Claire, with her street food background, enjoys leading classes such as Thai street food or curries of the world – anything where she can inject plenty of flavour into the recipes!

Everything in the kitchen is accessible and familiar. "We use domestic appliances rather than professional ones," explains Claire, "which we think is really important, so that you can then go home and recreate what you have made in the cookery school."

As well as their range of cooking courses, they also offer private hire for things such as parties (for adults and children), team-building experiences, community groups or even just a girls' night out! They head into schools, too, to teach Bristol's children how to incorporate their five-a-day into fun and exciting recipes, engaging them in cooking from an early age.

Whether it is making the perfect pasta, baking bread, spicing things up at the curry club, learning the basics for chicken, enjoying Saturday breakfast, creating classic cakes or magnificent macarons – The Little Kitchen is anything but little when it comes to flavours, creativity, inspiration and fun!

# Little Kitchen Cookery School

## MAR HOR

This is a spicy pork and pineapple dish we cook on our Thai street food course. People are always surprised by it as it is quite an unusual combination, but it is super-tasty! This makes an appetizer or nibbles for 2 people.

Preparation time: 10 minutes | Cooking time: 15 minutes | Serves 2.

### Ingredients

- 1 tsp ground nut oil
- 110g lean minced pork
- ½ small onion, finely chopped
- 1½ tbsp light brown sugar
- ½ tbsp fish sauce
- ½ tbsp Thai red curry paste
- ½ tbsp soy sauce
- ½ tbsp lime juice
- ½ tbsp chopped coriander
- 6 very thin slices fresh pineapple

### Method

Heat the oil in a frying pan on a medium to high heat. Add the minced pork, onion and brown sugar, stir and break the meat up with the back of a fork. Turn down the heat to medium and continue to fry until the meat starts to brown.

Combine the fish sauce, curry paste, soy sauce and lime juice in a cup. Once the meat has browned and the onions have caramelised, add the liquid in the cup and stir to coat the meat and onions, cooking until the liquid has evaporated.

Serve the pork on slices of the pineapple, sprinkle with coriander, roll and eat!

#### Adaptations

Try sprinkling with chopped peanuts and chilli for extra texture and heat!

Swap the pork mince for beef or turkey mince.

Swap the pork for quorn mince for a vegetarian option.

# West Country
# ON A PLATE

A deli at the front and a café at the back, The Mall Deli in historic Clifton Village is a true foodie paradise where local produce is championed, dishes are home-cooked and regulars have been coming back for decades.

Although Kate has been running the deli and café since 2010, The Mall Deli has actually been a key part of Clifton Village for 30 years. Bristol born and bred, Kate remembers childhood trips there to buy food with her mum. It's fair to say it has been through many a change over the years – at one point being linked by an archway to the butchers next door – but it has always been an important part of life for people in the village.

For Kate, having returned to the area after living in London for nearly a decade, taking over the deli was a privilege. The rich history of the village (which is older than Bristol itself), the elegant architecture, the iconic attractions and the plethora of diverse independent shops creates a mix that is difficult to match anywhere else in the country. She wanted to cherish what had made this long-standing business so special while evolving the product range, building relationships with local independent producers and engaging with customers old and new.

The team, which now consists of nearly 20 people, is perhaps what makes The Mall Deli such a success. "Our kitchen and deli teams work really hard to ensure that we have a wide variety of fresh home-made food every day, and that we keep our deli stocked up with wonderful goodies," says Kate. "And in the café, our waiting team and baristas are on first name terms with many of our regulars. They make fantastic coffees (using locally roasted Extract Coffee beans) from behind what is possibly the smallest coffee pod in the county!"

The welcoming interior is always busy with a real mix of people – its rustic feel and unpretentious ambience is testament to Kate's effort to make The Mall Deli a place where the whole community can feel at home. The deli at the front is an Aladdin's cave of goodies, shelves heaving with locally sourced products and fridges packed with home-made dishes.

"We love nothing more than discovering and meeting new local food producers who create fabulous produce, only otherwise available at local farmer's markets and small independents," explains Kate. Bristol Tea Company, Buxton Butchers, Reg the Veg, The Real Olive Co, Pullins Bakery and Zara's Chocolates are just a few of the trusted regional suppliers with whom she works.

And with Kate always on the hunt for new local produce, The Mall Deli is set to remain a little foodie haven in the heart of Clifton for many more years to come.

The Mall Deli

# The Mall Deli
# SMOKY AUBERGINE AND CHICKPEA SALAD

This is a really easy dish to prepare and is so versatile. It can be served as a salad accompaniment to pretty much anything (it's great for a BBQ), it can be served warm as a side to a lovely chunky chop or be a meal in itself with the addition of something like a bit of crumbled fresh goat's cheese.

Preparation time: 20 minutes | Cooking time: 20 minutes | Serves 4-6.

## Ingredients

1 medium aubergine

2 red peppers

1-2 tsp smoked paprika

2 400g cans of chickpeas

2 handfuls of fresh baby spinach

1 tbsp pumpkin seeds

1 tbsp sesame seeds

A handful of coriander or flat-leaf parsley

A squeeze of lemon juice

Olive oil, for drizzling

Salt and pepper

## Method

Preheat the oven to 175°C. Chop the aubergine and peppers into cubes and place into a baking tray that is large enough so that it all sits in one layer. Drizzle lightly with olive oil, sprinkle with 1-2 tsp smoked paprika (depending on how smoky you want it) and season with salt and pepper. Mix everything well to make sure all the veg is evenly coated, then roast the veg in the oven for about 20 minutes – you want it to be cooked through but still retain a bit of a bite.

Once the veg is out of the oven, drain and rinse the chickpeas, and add them to the baking tray. Wash the baby spinach, roughly chop it and add it to the tray (it will wilt slightly from the retained heat).

Toast the pumpkin and sesame seeds in a dry frying pan until lightly browned and add to the baking tray. Mix everything until evenly combined and leave to cool.

Once cool, mix through the chopped coriander and/or parsley, a squeeze of fresh lemon juice (to taste) and an additional drizzle of olive oil (if required).

# The Mall Deli
# CHOCOLATE STOUT CAKE

Inspired by various recipes we've tried out for chocolate Guinness cakes, this chocolate stout cake is universally popular with all our deli customers. We make this using locally brewed Wiper & True Milkshake or Porter. It is deliciously squidgy and moist, and works brilliantly as a tea-time cake or as a pudding, perhaps with some fresh berries on the side.

Preparation time: 20 minutes | Cooking time: 1 hour plus cooling time | Serves 10-12.

## Ingredients

### For the cake:

250ml Wiper & True Milkshake Stout or Porter (or other good-quality stout or porter)

250g unsalted butter, cut into cubes, plus a little extra for greasing the tin

75g cocoa powder

350g caster sugar

2 large free-range eggs

150ml natural yoghurt (we use Yeo Valley)

1 tsp vanilla extract (we use Little Pod)

200g plain flour

2½ tsp bicarbonate of soda

75g ground almonds

### For the topping:

250g mascarpone

60g icing sugar

A dash of vanilla bean paste or vanilla extract

## Method

### For the cake

Preheat the oven to 150°C. Grease and line a 23cm springform cake tin.

Pour the stout into a saucepan and heat on a moderate heat until simmering. Add the cubed butter and gently stir until melted. Once the butter has melted, add the cocoa powder and caster sugar to the pan. Whisk vigorously until the ingredients are well combined and the mixture is smooth, and leave on the hob to simmer for 5 minutes.

Whilst the stout mixture is simmering, beat the eggs, yoghurt and vanilla extract together until they are well combined. Sieve the flour and bicarbonate of soda into a large bowl, add the ground almonds and stir through to mix.

Take the saucepan off the heat. Add the egg mixture to the saucepan and fold together until well mixed. Make a well in the flour and pour and scrape the stout mix into the well. Fold everything together until smooth. If there are any lumps in the mix, break them down using a hand whisk.

Pour the mixture into the prepared cake tin and bake for approximately 1 hour. Test the cake with a skewer or knife – the cake is very moist so the skewer doesn't need to be completely dry or clean when it comes out, but it shouldn't have uncooked cake mixture stuck to it. Leave the cake to cool in its tin.

Once the cake is cool, take it out of its tin, remove the greaseproof paper and sit it on a serving plate.

### For the topping

Empty the mascarpone into a bowl and stir briefly to loosen. Sieve the icing sugar into the bowl and mix until smooth. If you have a hand-whisk or can do this in an electric mixer it will make the job quicker and ensure a smooth icing. Add a dash of vanilla bean paste or extract and mix through. Spread the mascarpone mix on top of the cake and decorate as you wish! We leave it plain and simple, resembling a glass of stout.

# Plates from the
# MEDITERRANEAN

Mediterranean food remains one of Bristol's favourite cuisines, and with Italian-inspired dishes being served up alongside delights from France and Spain at Manna in Westbury Park, it's easy to see why the city just can't get enough of those sunshine flavours.

Olly Gallery and Julian Faiello were not your typical restaurateurs when they opened their first eatery, Prego, in 2010. They both worked in the building trade and despite having a passion for European food – Julian's father is from Italy and Olly's father from France – they had always focused on eating in restaurants rather than running them! It was the building itself that inspired them and its potential as a gorgeous restaurant in the lovely Westbury Park area wouldn't leave their minds.

They opened Prego in 2010 to immediate success. In fact it was fully booked on opening night – which Olly describes as "a baptism of fire" as a head chef. Their business flourished from the outset, with diners falling in love with their classic approach to Italian dining.

When they were offered the opportunity to take over the restaurant over the road, they simply couldn't refuse. "It's such a great community and people here really love eating good-quality, locally-sourced food, so we wanted to continue to invest in the area and try something a bit different to Prego," explains Olly.

For their new restaurant, Manna, Olly and Julian wanted to celebrate the relaxed style of eating that they so loved about Europe. There are no strict rules at Manna. Perhaps you fancy an aperitif and a couple of tapas-style small plates? A locally sourced beer or a cocktail in the bar area? Or a traditional main course in the restaurant with a specially selected bottle of fine wine from their celebrated Italian wine list.

Listening to their customers is really important to Olly and Julian: "About seventy five percent of our customers are repeat visitors and we love to welcome them back week after week and hear what they want from their neighbourhood restaurant. We use local suppliers as much as we can (apart from the special ingredients we can only import from Italy) and celebrate Bristol's amazing producers. We keep the menu seasonal and change it regularly so there is always something new to try."

With both Prego and Manna now featured in The Good Food Guide, the regulars are also joined by people who seek them out from further afield.

You'll often see chefs running over the road between the two restaurants carrying armfuls of freshly picked veggies or meat from the local butcher. They have created a foodie hub in the heart of Westbury Park, which embraces all things delicious from Italy and beyond.

Manna

# Manna

# OVER-NIGHT LAMB SHOULDER WITH SLOW-COOKED CAULIFLOWER, ROASTED SWEET PEPPERS AND SALSA VERDE

Melt-in-the-mouth lamb is cooked with Mediterranean flavours in this winning family meal from Manna. The lamb needs to be prepared a day in advance.

Preparation time: 20 minutes | Cooking time: 6-7 hours plus resting overnight | Serves 4.

## Ingredients

1 small lamb shoulder

1 bunch of thyme

2 carrots, sliced

3 sticks of celery

1 head of garlic

375ml white wine

4 red Romano peppers

60g butter

2 onions, finely sliced

1 large cauliflower, finely sliced

1 bunch of parsley

1 bunch of mint

1 bunch of basil

1 bunch of dill

1 small tin of anchovies

1 small jar of capers

1 lemon, juice and zest

1 heaped tbsp Dijon mustard

A splash of red wine vinegar

Extra-virgin olive oil

Salt and pepper

## Method

Preheat the oven to 170°C. Place the lamb shoulder in a roasting tin with the thyme, sliced carrot and celery, some broken up garlic cloves and the white wine. Season with salt and pepper. Cover tightly with foil and place in the preheated oven for 5-6 hours. When done, turn off the oven and leave overnight. The next day remove the lamb from the stock and strain the stock to remove any fat. Retain the stock.

Preheat the oven to 200°C. The peppers can now be roasted in the hot oven until blackened all over. When black, put them in a bowl and cover in cling film. Leave the oven on.

Heat the butter in a large pan, add the sliced onions and four crushed garlic cloves and fry them in the butter until browned. Add the cauliflower to the browned onions and garlic and cook gently until the cauliflower starts to fall apart. Add a few ladles of the lamb stock to the cauliflower and then cook to reduce. Remove from the heat and keep warm.

Place the lamb back in to the hot oven for about 30 minutes to crisp up.

For the salsa verde, finely chop the herbs with the anchovies, capers and two cloves of garlic. When chopped, place in a bowl and add the lemon juice, mustard, vinegar and enough oil to make a think sauce. Taste it; it should be sharp and punchy!

Peel the blackened peppers, remove the seeds and tear into chunks.

For the finished dish, stir the zest of the lemon through the cauliflower and place in the middle of a plate. Pile on the crispy lamb, place some roasted peppers around and top with the salsa verde.

# More than OLIVES

The Glass Arcade in St Nicholas Market is a unique foodie venue and home to The Olive Works – Bristol's most mouth-watering array of healthy, fresh, locally-sourced yet globally-inspired salads.

Bristol's foodies will be familiar with The Olive Works – a long-standing salad bar that has been serving up Mediterranean-inspired olive mixes and fresh salads since 2009. It has been a firm favourite with regulars to St Nicholas Market for years, always keeping something new and exciting on the menu with seasonal goodies, flavourful home-made dressings, traditionally made Khobez flatbreads and the freshest local salads.

The Olive Works in its present form has evolved over the last 18 years. The story goes back to 1998, when Ben and partner Karin set up The Real Olive Company and began importing the finest Greek olives into Bristol and preparing and marinating them in time-honoured ways. A new concept in Bristol at the time, people were blown away by the flavour of the produce.

Based in the lovely surroundings of The Glass Arcade in St Nicholas Market, Ben, responding to consumer demand decided to introduce lunch foods to go. At the same time demand from far and wide to wholesale the olives to food businesses (from pubs and restaurants to delis and farm shops) had grown and the decision was taken to separate The Real Olive Company wholesale business from St Nicks.

Ben focused on the wholesale business while Roger joined to run St Nicks, which was renamed The Olive Works.

Ben and Roger still rely on The Real Olive Company for their incredible olives and antipasti products, but their focus is well and truly on the salad selection, which usually comprises between 12 and 15 dishes adorning the counter each day. An enticing display of colours, textures and aromas, The Olive Works salads pay homage to the bounty of fresh ingredients available around Bristol.

"Provenance is really important at The Olive Works," explains Roger. "We work with local suppliers to get the best-tasting quality ingredients, from our free-range chicken and locally farmed lamb to all the fresh leaves and vegetables. We also make everything from scratch, right down to our pesto."

There is a lot of emphasis on Middle Eastern flavours, as well as Mediterranean, with the traditionally made Khobez flatbreads being one of their most famous products. Although the dishes change regularly, there are some recipes that are so popular Roger and Ben daren't remove them from the selection! The Pecorino cheese salad is one of those winning combinations, which is why they have chosen to share their famous recipe for it in this book. Enjoy!

The Olive Works

MEAL DEAL
•Salad box +drink £5
•Salad box +chicken or lamb £5,5

DRINKS
•Water Still/Sparkling
•San Pellegrino

Falafel

# The Olive Works
## PECORINO SALAD

This is one of the best-sellers at The Olive Works. It is bright and colourful and a lovely summer salad when tomatoes are at their best. We have included our vegan pesto recipe here, but you can simply add 20g Parmesan to it for this lovely cheese-based salad!

Preparation time: 20 minutes | Serves 6-8.

## Ingredients

### For the pesto:

30g basil leaves

20g ground almonds

½ garlic clove

2 tbsp extra virgin olive oil

Sea salt and cracked black pepper

### For the salad:

12 large ripe vine tomatoes

150g pecorino cheese

½ medium red onion, quartered and finely sliced

50g pesto (see above)

100g baby spinach, roughly chop half the spinach

Extra virgin olive oil, to dress

## Method

### For the pesto

Start by making the pesto. Blitz all the ingredients together in a food processor until smooth. Season with sea salt, cracked black pepper and a pinch of sugar to suit. This is our vegan pesto recipe, but you can add 20g Parmesan to it, if you like.

### For the salad

Chop the vine tomatoes into 2cm chunks and scatter in the bottom of a bowl. Remove the rind from the Pecorino and cut into broad shavings using a vegetable peeler. Add half the Pecorino shavings, finely sliced red onion, pesto, the roughly chopped spinach and mix together with the tomatoes.

Dress the top of the tomato mixture with the remaining half of the spinach leaves, scatter over the rest of the pecorino shavings and drizzle extra virgin olive oil to suit.

# Raising the STEAKS

Beef reigns supreme at The Ox, where steaks are cooked to absolute perfection and the Sunday Roast is regarded as one of the finest available in Bristol...

With two successful speakeasy bars under their belts a restaurant was a natural progression for the Hyde & Co team, and when they decide to embark on a new venture, they don't do things by halves. Having breathed a bit of New York style into the city's drinking scene with Hyde & Co and The Milk Thistle, they spent a long time waiting for the right project to sink their teeth into next. The derelict space in a basement on Corn Street was their perfect opportunity. They were won over by the potential in the architecture and original features, and set about turning the unloved space into an awe-inspiring restaurant.

With their combined experience covering the restaurant industry and managing building projects, the three got to work transforming the neglected basement into an award-winning steak restaurant. Inspired by restaurants in London and New York, it was their attention to every detail that set The Ox apart from anything else on offer in Bristol at the time.

"Great ideas are one thing," muses Nathan, "but you need great staff to turn them into a reality, and that is what made The Ox into something special." Head chef Todd Francis has been key in making The Ox a stand-out dining destination – something which hasn't gone unnoticed by The Bristol Good Food Guide, who awarded them Bristol's Best Steak in 2015. It's not all about the steaks though, with small plates, charcuterie and other classic main courses also on offer, as well as delectable desserts and lovely cheese boards. Their Sunday roasts are renowned as being among the best available in the city – roast beef rib-eye is the cut of choice, although the crisp belly of pork and fillet of hake are also understandably popular. There is always a carefully considered vegetarian dish on the menu, too, of course!

The Ox is a place where the wine is as good as the steaks and plenty of cocktails are shaken and stirred at the bar. Whether you want a deep red, a light, crisp white or a classic cocktail, the bartenders take the drinks list very seriously indeed. With such attention to detail, The Ox has been a successful addition to Bristol's vibrant food scene – so successful in fact that the team have launched a second site in Clifton, so more people will now be able to sample those sensational steaks and Sunday lunches.

# The Ox
## BBQ GLAZED RIBS

You will need to start this recipe two days before you plan to serve them, as the ribs need to marinate overnight and then chill again overnight once braised. Although it may seem time-consuming, the incredible flavour is well worth the time spent.

Preparation time: 10 minutes, plus 2 nights of marinating and chilling
Cooking time: 3 hours, plus finishing off on the BBQ | Serves 6.

## Ingredients

3 racks of pork ribs

**For the marinade:**

½ cup light brown sugar

1 tbsp Maldon sea salt

¾ tbsp smoked paprika

1 tbsp garlic powder

1 tsp allspice powder

1¼ litres apple juice

350ml dark ale

1 onion

85ml cider vinegar

18ml Worcester sauce

## Method

### Day 1

Blitz all marinade ingredients together and pour over the ribs. Cover and place in the fridge to marinate overnight.

### Day 2

Preheat the oven to 120°C. Place the ribs in a roasting tray with the marinade and cover with foil. Place in the preheated oven and braise for about 3 hours, until the meat is just about to fall off the bone – too much and the ribs will disintegrate on the bbq, not enough and they will be tough. Allow to cool and then refrigerate overnight.

### Day 3

Skim off the fat from the top of the pan. Pass the liquid through a sieve into a saucepan and reduce over medium heat until the sauce coats the back of a spoon. It should be rich and luscious. This is your glaze. Cut the ribs into portions and barbeque them over charcoal until charred and smokey. Add the rib portions to the warm glaze pan to coat and serve immediately.

# The Ox
# SALTED CARAMEL
# AND CHOCOLATE DELICE

A luxurious dessert from The Ox – a buttery base coated in layers of chocolate and salted caramel. You need to allow it to set for 6 hours over the course of the recipe, so make this recipe ahead of time.

Preparation time: 30 minutes, plus 6 hours setting time | Cooking time: 30 minutes | Serves 8.

## Ingredients

**For the delice base:**

100g butter

100g caster sugar

100g ground almonds

100g flour

7g salt

**For the chocolate layer:**

280ml full-fat milk

650ml double cream

4 eggs, beaten

680g chocolate (70%), broken into pieces

**For the salted caramel layer:**

225g dark brown sugar

300ml double cream

225g butter, chopped

2 gelatine leaves, soaked in cold water

Salt, to taste

**For the chocolate glaze:**

225ml water

262g caster sugar

83g cocoa powder

163ml double cream

5 gelatine leaves, soaked in cold water

60g chocolate (70%), broken into pieces

## Method

**For the delice base**

Preheat the oven to 180°C. Line a 25cm brownie pan with parchment (preferably spring-form or loose-bottom). Melt the butter and mix with the dry ingredients. Press into the prepared pan.

Bake in the preheated oven until it is a deep, golden brown. Take out and press lightly with a spatula to flatten the base.

**For the chocolate layer**

Heat the milk and cream until just starting to boil. Place the eggs in one bowl and the chocolate into another. Pour the milk and cream mixture onto the eggs and whisk, then pour the mixture over the chocolate and stir to combine fully. Pour over the base and refrigerate for about 3 hours until fully set.

**For the salted caramel layer**

Place all the ingredients except the gelatine and salt into a pan and bring to the boil. Squeeze out the water from the gelatine leaves. Whisk the soaked gelatine into the mixture and season with salt. Pour onto the chocolate layer, about ½cm in depth.

**For the chocolate glaze**

Place all the ingredients except the gelatine and chocolate into a pan and bring to the boil, whisking to emulsify. Remove from the heat. Squeeze out the water from the gelatine leaves and add the soaked gelatine and chocolate to the pan, stirring to disperse. Pour over the salted caramel layer, about 3mm in depth, and leave to set for about 3 hours. Portion into eight generous pieces to serve.

# Jamon, sherry and
# SPANISH STYLE

Post-work pintxos and a glass of sherry, plates of the finest jamón Iberico, late night Latin-inspired cocktails and dancing... Pata Negra has brought a taste of Spanish life to the centre of Bristol.

Literally meaning 'black hoof', Pata Negra celebrates the iconic Spanish Iberico ham – the familiar silhouette of the prized acorn-eating Iberian pig at the entrance lets diners know that they are in for an authentic taste of Spain in this tapas bar. The dream of food-lover Jo Clerc, Pata Negra came about when she shared her idea for an authentic tapas bar with the team behind Hyde & Co, The Milk Thistle and The Ox. Inspired by their success and with a passion for pintxos and love of Spanish culture, Jo went into business with Nathan, Jason and Kevin, and together they set about turning Jo's vision into a reality.

It was a big undertaking and the team spent a long time getting the feel of the place just right – the three floors would provide space to have a bar and kitchen, a dance floor and a private room. They wanted to capture the laid-back spirit of Spain and have space for people to enjoy the laid-back vibes, whether it be to eat, drink, dance or just generally relax, was vital.

Today, the vibrant space bustles with people from midday to midnight. People enjoy bottles of robust Spanish reds or crisp white wines to wash down small plates of cured meats, marinated olives, salted almonds, croquetas, meatballs, boquerones, tortilla or Spanish cheeses. It's also a popular spot to enjoy sherry – the team admit they are big fans of it and have a selection that is sure to contain something to match your mood (or food). The sherry list is always evolving and lots of the regular customers take advantage of the happy hour where you can sample three pintxos along with your fino for a bargain price.

Later in the day the atmosphere amplifies as the chatter gets louder and Latin-inspired cocktails begin to flow – time to hit the dancefloor upstairs in Noche Negra. Bristolians have taken this little slice of España to their hearts and embraced the intoxicating charm of eating, drinking and letting their hair down Spanish-style.

Pata Negra

# Pata Negra
# CROQUETAS DE JAMÓN

This recipe makes enough for four greedy tapas fans and is one of those true Spanish classics that can transport you to sunnier climes in a mouthful.

Preparation time: 15 minutes, plus 30 minutes cooling | Cooking time: 20 minutes | Serves 4.

## Ingredients

500ml milk

A pinch of freshly grated nutmeg

60g unsalted butter

125g Serrano ham, diced

85g plain flour, plus extra for dusting

2 eggs, beaten with a splash of milk

150g panko breadcrumbs

Oil, for deep-frying

Salt and white pepper

## Method

Place the milk into a pan and add the freshly grated nutmeg. Heat the milk to a simmer.

Meanwhile, melt the butter in a separate good-sized, sturdy pan until it foams. Add the diced Serrano ham and fry for 3 minutes. Add the flour to the butter and Serrano to make a roux and cook for a further 5 minutes, stirring continuously until smooth.

Add the hot milk, a little at a time, until it has formed a smooth, thick paste. Season with salt and pepper to taste. Transfer the mixture to a lightly greased tray to cool, covering the surface with cling film so that it doesn't form a skin.

When it is cold, shape the mixture into 50g croquetas. Dust the croquetas in flour, then roll the croquetas in the beaten egg mixture, making sure you allow any excess egg to drip off. Finally, roll the croquetas in the breadcrumbs.

Heat the oil for deep-frying to 165°C and deep-fry until golden and hot all the way through; about 5 minutes. Remove using a slotted spoon and drain on kitchen paper. Devour!

# A 21ST CENTURY BAKERY

Pinkmans is a celebration of everything that made traditional bakeries great, while challenging conceptions of what a bakery on the modern high street can be… a cocktail with your cake perhaps?

Pinkmans is a place where old meets new. Traditions are cherished while new ideas are explored. At its heart is a bakery – the oven forms the very soul of the business, and it is from the onsite oven where bread starts emerging from 8am.

Opening its doors in December 2015, Pinkmans is a collaboration between long-time bakers and pastry chefs Steven Whibley, Troels Bendix and Michael Engler. In Steven's words, the business is an expression of what a modern high street bakery can be. "The buzz and energy at Pinkmans comes from making and baking everything in the same space as we sell it. In most places where you buy your bread, the bakers are non-existent, being packed off in some production facility that may make things easier but loses the excitement and passion that comes with wild yeast baking, Pinkmans is our attempt to change that."

It might not look like a typical bakery but at the heart of the business are bakers… and lots and lots of baking. Pizzas, fresh bread, sandwiches, cakes and tarts are all eaten around sharing tables, which contributes to the irresistible buzz and vibrant atmosphere. The team are certainly passionate about what they do, always eager to help and engage with the customers, there's a warmth to the atmosphere that has nothing to do with the baker's oven.

What makes this place different is its innovative approach to the bakery business. Open from 8am until 10pm, they are fully licenced and serve fabulous cocktails and spritzers alongside coffee, tea and freshly squeezed juices. The upmarket cafeteria is centred around its open bakery kitchen with wood-fired oven, and food emerges onto a stunning 6-metre copper counter to be served to diners in the convivial surroundings of the 70-seater communal dining hall.

Pinkmans are hugely supportive of local suppliers, using Bristol-based Buxton Butchers for their meat, French Garden for their fruit and vegetables, flour from Shipton Mill, spelt flour from Sharpham Park, Grape & Grind for wine and a selection of local breweries for their eclectic beer and cider selection.

Their speciality sourdough, made with wild yeast starters, is renowned and is one of the reasons why their breads, pastries and pizzas are so utterly irresistible. However when it comes to something that people just can't get enough of, it's hard to beat the sour-dough-nuts! With ever-changing products keeping things fresh and interesting, this new generation of bakery is something truly inspired.

# Pinkmans
# APPLE CRUMBLE CAKE WITH CINNAMON ICE CREAM

This is an old favourite that works well hot or cold, eaten alone or even better we think served warm with cinnamon ice cream. The crumble is a great crumble topping to bake on top of muffins or sweet brioches, too.

Preparation time: 15 minutes | Cooking time: 1 hour 40 minutes, plus 5 hours infusing | Serves 4.

## Ingredients

**For the cinnamon ice cream:**

1 litre whole milk

75g fresh ginger, peeled and finely chopped

10g ground cinnamon

1 vanilla pod, split

½ orange, zest

8 egg yolks

125g light soft brown sugar

**For the apple purée:**

4 Granny Smith apples, cored and finely chopped

30g caster sugar

2g malic acid (available online)

**For the wholemeal crumble:**

250g wholemeal flour

100g plain flour

100g porridge oats

80g light brown sugar

2g cinnamon

1g ground nutmeg

1g clove powder

160g butter

**For the cake:**

2 Bramley apples, peeled, cored and diced

50g pecans, chopped

50g sultanas

50g dried apple, chopped

30ml brandy

10ml lemon juice

60g granulated sugar

160g Demerara sugar

2 medium eggs

150g unsalted butter, melted

200g plain flour

6g baking powder

3g salt

3g ground cinnamon

2g ground nutmeg

1g clove powder

## Method

### For the cinnamon ice cream

Place the milk in a pan and bring to a simmer. Remove from the heat and add the ginger, cinnamon, vanilla pod and orange zest. Cover and leave to infuse for 60 minutes. Then pass through a fine sieve to remove the aromatics.

Return the milk mixture to the heat and bring to a simmer. Whisk together the egg yolks and sugar in a bowl and then pour the hot milk mixture on to the yolks and sugar and whisk to combine. Return to the pan and continue to cook on a gentle heat, stirring continuously, until the mixture coats the back of a spoon. Remove from the heat and pass through a fine sieve. Chill the mixture in the fridge for 2 hours.

Pour the chilled mixture into a plastic container with a secure lid and place in the freezer. Remove the mixture every 1 hour and stir well to encourage an even freezing and reduce ice crystals. Repeat the process until the mixture is of a soft-scoop ice cream consistency.

### For the apple purée

Place the apples in a pan with the caster sugar and malic acid and cover with a lid. Place on the stove and cook on a medium heat for 10 minutes, then remove the lid and continue cooking until soft and broken down. Purée in a food processor and, if possible, pass through a fine sieve. Set aside.

### For the wholemeal crumble

Preheat the oven to 170°C. Combine the dry ingredients in a food mixer fitted with the paddle attachment and then add the butter and rub to a crumb. Place in a baking tray and bake the mix for about 45 minutes, rubbing through the mixture every 15 minutes to avoid large lumps. Set aside.

### For the cake

Preheat the oven to 190°C. Grease and line a 25cm square cake tin.

Place the diced apples, chopped pecans, sultanas, chopped dried apple into a mixing bowl, then add the brandy and lemon juice and leave to macerate for 30 minutes.

In a food mixer fitted with the whisk attachment, whip the sugars and the eggs for 4 minutes. Then add the melted butter, then the flour, baking powder, salt, cinnamon, nutmeg and clove powder. Finally, add the macerated fruit and nuts.

Bake for about 40 minutes or until firm to the touch and golden. Then cover the top with the apple purée and top with the wholemeal crumble. Allow to cool, then portion and serve with the cinnamon ice cream.

# Pinkmans
# CORNBREAD WITH SMOKED SALMON AND AVOCADO SALSA

This is a very popular dish on our breakfast menu. We think the flavours and colours combine beautifully here, although the cornbread is a wonderfully versatile partner also combining well with eggs, bacon and making delicious savoury muffins to be eaten on their own. We bake the cornbread in loaf tins and slice it, but for home-cooking, we have amended it here to make six 100g muffins, as muffin tins and cases are more common in the home kitchen. The cornbread can be baked the day before and refreshed in the oven, or the mix can be made in advance and baked off in the morning.

Preparation time: 40 minutes, plus 1 hour chilling | Cooking time: 25 minutes | Serves 6.

## Ingredients

### For the cornbread:

150g plain flour

1 tbsp baking powder

1 tbsp caster sugar

4g salt

110g fine polenta

70g mature cheddar, grated

4 spring onions, finely chopped

1 red chilli, deseeded and finely chopped

250g buttermilk

2 large eggs

60ml olive oil

80ml honey

### For the avocado salsa:

1 ripe avocado

1 tomato, deseeded and finely chopped

Red onion and parsley, finely chopped, to taste

1 lemon, juice and zest, to taste

Olive oil, to taste

Pinch of salt & pepper

### To serve:

Smoked salmon

Crème fraîche

## Method

### For the cornbread

Preheat the oven to at 190°C. Combine the dry ingredients with the grated cheese, finely chopped spring onions and chilli in a mixing bowl. In another bowl, lightly whisk the eggs and combine the olive oil, honey and buttermilk. Using a whisk, incorporate the wet ingredients into the dry ingredients and mix to a smooth paste. Then chill for at least an hour to let the polenta absorb some of the moisture. Spoon into six lightly greased muffin cases and bake for 25 minutes or until golden and cooked through.

### For the avocado and tomato salsa

Dice rather than mash the ripe avocado and combine it with the finely chopped tomato, red onion, parsley, lemon zest, juice, a pinch of salt & pepper and a few drops of virgin olive oil.

### To serve

Cut the cornbread muffin on a slant and pile on the avocado salsa, top with smoked salmon (the best you can afford), and serve with a side of crème fraîche.

# Dining on the
# DOCKSIDE

Modern European cuisine in a wonderfully Bristolian setting, riverstation's two floors of waterside dining have been welcoming back regulars for 18 years.

Looking at the bright, modern exterior of this beautifully designed space, it's hard to imagine that riverstation was once Bristol's river police station. When it opened to the public in 1997 it won instant acclaim for its design, and it's fair to say, 18 years later, riverstation feels as contemporary today as it did back then.

Still independently owned, riverstation achieves that elusive mix between long-standing class and continually moving with the times. Customers return time and time again – some of whom have been repeat visitors for over a decade – and they love that they are still greeted by the familiar faces of staff members who have remained as loyal to riverstation as they have.

For the team at both the waterside bar+kitchen and the first floor restaurant, the service is as important as the food. Whether it's a laid-back lunch on the terrace or a refined three-course dinner, it's the whole dining experience that makes riverstation such a special part of the Bristol dining scene – from start to finish, nothing is too much trouble for the team.

As far as the food is concerned, the menus can change daily as they are dictated by the best produce the chefs can get their hands on each day. They have been working with

their suppliers for many years, so they know that they are always getting the best of everything – from meat and fish to Bristol-grown produce, and even the tea and coffee from local suppliers.

In the kitchen everything is made from scratch, whether it's baking their own bread or making their own ice cream. In the first floor restaurant these ingredients are showcased in creative and interesting dishes that sit as beautifully on the plate as they do on the palate. Alongside the impressive à la carte options, the restaurant also offers extraordinarily good value set menus for different times of day, exemplifying the focus on offering really good food at affordable prices.

A comprehensive and carefully selected wine list has a New World and Italian focus, and there is also a great selection of locally sourced beers and ciders. The range of spirits is also popular as they always try to opt for alternatives to the mainstream offerings, leading to some really interesting cocktails.

On the terrace of the bar+kitchen, people sit back and watch the boats bobbing past. From morning coffee and home-made cakes right through to seasonal suppers and bottles of wine as the sun goes down, there couldn't be a more relaxing place to enjoy Bristol's irresistible waterside charm.

riverstation

# *riverstation*
# BEETROOT GAZPACHO

This recipe is great for the summer and a nice twist on the classic gazpacho; it's refreshing, easy to make and a beautiful colour thanks to the addition of beetroot. You need to make this recipe the day before you plan to serve it.

Preparation time: 20 minutes, plus chilling overnight | Cooking time: 30 minutes | Serves 2.

## Ingredients

*100g raw beetroot*

*1 garlic clove*

*½ cucumber*

*1 red pepper*

*150g ripe tomatoes*

*10g sliced red onion*

*2g basil leaf*

*2g coriander leaf*

*5ml sherry vinegar*

*5g tomato purée*

*3g sugar*

*3g salt*

*1g ground black pepper*

*15ml olive oil*

**To serve:**

*Crème fraîche and toasted almond flakes*

## Method

First boil the raw beetroot, skin on, in slightly salted water until the centre has softened and can be pierced with a skewer or fork without too much resistance. Drain off the water, allow to cool and peel the skin.

Next grate the beetroot and garlic, then cut the cucumber, red pepper and tomatoes into rough 2½cm chunks. You can now add all of the ingredients together (apart from the crème fraîche and toasted almond flakes) and leave in a sealable tub in the fridge overnight, this will allow the flavours to marinate together and work their magic.

The next day blitz the mixture in a liquidiser until smooth and keep in the fridge until ready to serve. Best served with a dollop of crème fraîche and a sprinkle of toasted almond flakes.

# Best of the
# BRUNCH

The vision of three passionate foodies, Rosemarino has brought a touch of relaxed Italian charm to Bristol's food scene, as well as some of the greatest breakfasts for miles around.

The shared vision of Tony De Brito, Sam Fryer and Mirco Bertoldi, Rosemarino burst onto the Bristol food scene in 2010. The three had met working in the food and drink industry and it soon became clear that they were all passionate about doing something new and exciting. "It was something we talked about a lot," remembers Mirco, "and I suppose it was me who got the ball rolling when I came across the Clifton premises." When he presented the idea to the others, it soon became apparent that their dream could be a reality, and from that moment on, they have never looked back.

It was a fresh concept in Bristol at the time – combining casual Italian dining and all-day brunch with a really relaxed but professional vibe. You won't find the menu divided into starters and main courses. The idea is to have less restriction around the food – simply choose small plates or large plates, eat them to yourself or share them, it's up to you.

Menu inspiration is taken from all over Italy but there are hints of Mirco's Italian heritage peppering the menu, from his father's home-cured speck, which is sent from Trentino, to desserts made from generations-old family recipes. However, it is clear that the Rosemarino team put as much passion into sourcing local products (such as their Bristol-grown salad leaves) as they do in making sure their homemade pasta, which comes in all sorts of inventive, exciting flavours is prepared fresh every day.

Having been voted The Best Italian in Bristol every year since 2012, it's interesting that for many people, Rosemarino is also synonymous with breakfast (they won The Best Breakfast for three consecutive years, too). Rosemarino has become a renowned destination for weekend brunch, so much so that customers have to book in advance in order to get a table. The famous homemade focaccia (which is made fresh each day to a special recipe) is served with the breakfast, and this delicious bread alone has fans across the city.

A small yet quirky wine list is available. It's all Italian but aims to provide a refreshing change to the usual offerings, with unusual grape varieties and blends from some wonderful small producers. Another import from Mirco's father in Trentino, the homemade honey grappa, also wins over many a customer!

"It's been a really positive journey," says Tony, "summed up by our happy family of staff who bring Rosemarino to life each day."

# Rosemarino
# ARANCINI 'MELANZANE PARMIGIANA'

Tomato arancini with smoked aubergine and mozzarella. This dish encapsulates what we are all about at Rosemarino. We take inspiration from traditional regional Italian recipes, like the Sicilian arancini and put our twist on it. This time we took the ingredients from another classic, Melanzane Parmigiana from Campania to create our very own Rosemarino classic.

Preparation time: 40 minutes | Cooking time: 50 minutes | Serves 4.

## Ingredients

**For the tomato stock:**

1 large onion
1 head celery
2 carrots
1 leek
1 sprig of thyme
2 bay leaves
1 tsp fennel seeds
1 tsp black peppercorns
1 litre water
1 tin of chopped tomatoes

**For the smoked aubergine purée:**

2 aubergines
50ml olive oil
1 lemon, juice
A pinch of cumin
Salt and pepper

**For the arancini:**

2 tbsp olive oil
1 red onion, finely chopped
2 garlic cloves, finely chopped
200g arborio rice
A knob of butter
100ml white wine
600ml tomato stock
1 jar of passata
½ bunch of basil
8 baby mozzarella balls
50g Parmesan, grated
300g dried breadcrumbs
150g flour
3 eggs, beaten
Salt and pepper
Vegetable oil, for deep-frying
Semi-dried cherry tomatoes, to serve

## Method

**For the tomato stock**

Roughly chop the vegetables and put in a saucepan along with the herbs, spices and water. Bring to the boil, then add the chopped tomatoes and simmer for 15 minutes.

**For the smoked aubergine purée**

Preheat the oven to 200°C. Roast the aubergines in the oven until the skins begin to split and crack. Place in a bowl, cover with cling film and allow to steam for 20 minutes. When the aubergines are soft, peel the skins and place the flesh in a blender. Blitz with the olive oil, lemon juice and cumin until smooth. Season well.

**For the arancini**

Heat a large, heavy-based pan on high heat. Add the olive oil, onion and garlic and cook until softened. Add the rice and butter, turn to a medium heat and cook until the butter has melted, stirring constantly. Add the wine and bubble away for a few minutes, continuing to stir regularly.

Start adding the stock, little by little, ensuring the rice absorbs each ladleful of liquid before adding the next. Keep stirring regularly as this releases the starch from the rice, making it easier to shape later. Continue until the rice is al dente, about 15 minutes.

Add the passata and season, and cook for a further 5 minutes on low heat until the rice is cooked through. Pour the risotto onto a tray and allow to cool. When cool, add the chopped basil and divide into eight equal balls. Stuff each ball with a baby mozzarella ball in the centre and wrap the risotto around it. Shape into cones.

Preheat the oven to 180°C. Mix the Parmesan and breadcrumbs together. Place the flour, eggs and breadcrumbs in three separate shallow bowls. Dredge each cone in flour, then place in the egg and finally the breadcrumbs, ensuring each cone is completely covered. Heat the oil for deep-frying to 180°C and deep-fry the arancini until golden brown. Transfer to the preheated oven and continue to cook for 5 minutes. Serve 2 cones per portion with some of the purée and semi-dried cherry tomatoes.

# A pinch
# OF SALT

Situated just outside the city centre, Salt is a new addition to Bristol's thriving café scene which is adding a little extra flavour to the menu with a sprinkling of music, art and film thrown in.

Tucked away slightly off the beaten track, yet only a stone's throw from Bristol's centre, Salt is a bright and airy yet cosy and stylish café where there is always something happening. It opened in August 2015, a joint venture between Alice Mahtani and Alan Strawbridge, who were united by a passion for good food and drink, along with a love of music, film and all kinds of other arty events.

Alice had experience in working in catering as well as the arts before she became a full-time mum, and Alan's career had seen him working as a musician, an events organiser and in web design. Add their love for cooking to the mix and between them they had the skill-set to create something a little bit different.

Their shared vision for Salt emerged and they began by getting their menu just right... home-style food made with the best local ingredients they can source. It has always been vital for Alan and Alice that they don't cut corners on their produce – they opt for ethically sourced meat, organic produce where they can, fresh and seasonal veggies, and everything from as close to home as possible.

The freshly prepared sandwiches quickly became famous in the area thanks to the emphasis on quality. What can be better than a classic British cheese, ham and chutney sandwich when the ham is free-range Wiltshire ham, the cheese is top-quality cheddar and the chutney is made in-house? Gluten-free bread is available and vegans are well catered for too.

Breakfasts, pastries, frittatas, quiches, soups and salads are all freshly made on the premises ready for people to enjoy in the friendly surrounds or to take away when they're in a rush. The enormous sausage rolls have achieved local fame, as have the salted caramel and chocolate cake and the sugar-free brownies, which nobody can quite believe are sugar-free! Since everything is made in the kitchen, freshness is guaranteed – right down to the home-made pickles, jams and even ketchup.

With Alan's history in organising events, it's no surprise that there is always something happening at Salt. "We host a weekly live music night and regular film nights, as well as being a welcoming destination for community groups, birthday parties and social gatherings, " he explains. And with plenty of new ideas up their sleeves, Salt Café is set to welcome plenty more events into their unique little eatery in the future.

Salt Café

salt local, ethical food & drink

# Salt Café
# SALTED CARAMEL BROWNIES

These brownies are one of Salt Café's best-sellers. The sweet and salty combination of salted caramel never fails to please the palate! The salted caramel will make enough for two batches of brownies, but it's worth making this amount as it keeps in the fridge for a couple of weeks and also freezes well.

Preparation time: 10 minutes | Cooking time: 40 minutes, plus 15 minutes freezing | Serves 8.

## Ingredients

**For the salted caramel:**

375g caster sugar

450ml double cream

75g unsalted butter

2-3 tsp sea salt

**For the brownies:**

315g unsalted butter

625g caster sugar

160g unsweetened cocoa powder

1 tsp pure vanilla extract

1 tsp salt

6 eggs

160g plain flour

## Method

**For the salted caramel**

Heat the sugar in a heavy-bottomed saucepan over a medium heat. Once it starts to melt swirl the sugar into the liquid areas of the pan. Do not leave the pan unattended as it can burn very quickly. Meanwhile, gently warm the cream in a separate pan.

Once the sugar is melted and amber, remove the pan from the heat. Gradually add the cream and whisk. It will bubble a lot – be careful, as it's very hot, so try not to let it splash your skin. Add the butter and whisk in. If the sugar solidifies, simply return the pan to a medium heat.

Pour the caramel through a sieve into a heatproof bowl and leave to cool. Stir in the salt

**For the brownies**

Preheat the oven to 180°C (160°C fan) and line a 20 x 30cm brownie tin with greaseproof paper.

Combine the butter, sugar and cocoa in a medium heatproof bowl. Either place the bowl over a pan of simmering water or microwave it for 2-3 minutes (stirring once during cooking), until the butter has melted, mix well. Leave to cool until the mixture is warm not hot; it will look quite gritty.

Add the vanilla and salt. Add the eggs one at a time, beating after each addition. When the batter looks thick, shiny and well blended, add the flour and beat until you cannot see it any longer, then beat for 30 seconds more.

Fill the prepared tin halfway, spread over a thick layer of salted caramel, and top with the rest of the brownie batter. Drizzle extra caramel on top.

Bake in the preheated oven for 30 minutes until a cocktail stick plunged into the centre emerges slightly moist with batter. Let cool completely. Put the brownies in the freezer for 15 minutes or so before cutting, otherwise they are likely to break. Cut into 8 pieces to serve.

# Exploring the SOUKS

Taking inspiration from countries across the Middle East and North Africa, as well as lots of delicious bites from the Eastern Mediterranean, Soukitchen serves up flavours that really pack a punch...

When it comes to food that is made to be shared, and flavours that really leave your tastebuds tingling, it's hard to beat the souks of the Middle East and North Africa. It was these havens of local produce, aromatic spices and fresh food that inspired Darren and Ella Lovell when they decided to open Soukitchen.

The husband and wife team opened the first Soukitchen in Southville in 2010, followed by the premises in Clifton in 2014. With a Bristol Good Food Award for Best Mediterranean in 2014 and 2015, it's clear that their delicious food was quickly embraced by Bristolians.

"Eating out in the Middle East is a way of life", enthuses Ella, and Soukitchen are attempting to recreate that passion, authenticity and atmosphere right here in Bristol. They aim to make every diner feel relaxed as soon as they arrive. "Every customer is a member of the family the moment they walk through the door."

The welcome may win them over immediately, but it's the mouth-watering flavours that keep customers coming back time and time again. Honest, creative and inventive is how Darren and Ella describe their menu. It's food for sharing, food with heart, food that makes you want to roll up your sleeves and get stuck in.

Brunch, lunch and dinner are served in both restaurants – for brunch choose "The Local" (traditional full English ) or opt for Middle Eastern specialities like Shakshouka topped with merguez sausage and feta, go for a vibrant mezze selection or chargrilled skewers for lunch, and tuck into their famous ghalieh mahi (Persian fish curry) for dinner.

For executive chef Darren, food should tell a story. He loves to take inspiration from foreign shores while using local suppliers for his ingredients, celebrating provenance, seasonality and independent producers. This in turn leads to top-quality food emerging from the kitchen, so it wasn't surprising when The Times named Soukitchen one of the country's best cheap eateries, something that the team are incredibly proud of.

Their adventurous wine list is a breath of fresh air, too. They champion fine wines from Turkey, Greece and the Balkans, encouraging diners to try their Peloponnese house wine, the Moroccan lager or an inventive cocktail – think Turkish apple tea mojito or pomegranate and rose gin and tonic.

The Clifton restaurant also has its own souk shop, selling those hard-to-come-by ingredients – perfect for trying their delicious recipe overleaf!

WALNUT
BAKLAVA
£2.95

# Soukitchen
# BAHARAT ROASTED DUCK MUJADDARA AND PEKMEZ

You can buy some of the special ingredients for this in our Clifton shop, such as the Baharat spice mix and the grape pekmez. Marinate the duck the night before, if you have time.

Preparation time: 15 minutes, plus 2-12 hours marinating | Cooking time: 1 hour 15 minutes | Serves 4.

## Ingredients

**For the duck:**

4 duck legs

1 tbsp Baharat spice mix

6 garlic cloves, peeled

1 orange, quartered

2 sprigs of thyme

1 large red chilli, split and deseeded

3 tbsp olive oil

20 seedless grapes

1 tbsp honey

3 tbsp grape pekmez

100ml chicken stock

Salt

**For the mujaddara:**

300g puy lentils

200ml vegetable oil

3 large white onions, thinly sliced

1 tbsp olive oil

2 tsp cumin seeds

½ lemon, peel

2 tsp ground allspice

2 bay leaves

A pinch of salt

200g good-quality basmati rice, washed

**To garnish:**

Pomegranate seeds

A handful of flat leaf parsley

## Method

### For the duck

Score the skin of the duck legs with a sharp knife. Be careful not to score the flesh. Combine the Baharat spice mix, garlic, orange, thyme, chilli and olive oil in a large bowl, add the duck legs and mix well. Leave in the fridge for at least 2 hours, or overnight for best results.

Preheat the oven to 190°C. Place the duck legs skin-side up in a small deep-sided roasting tray along with its marinade. Season with salt and roast in the preheated oven for 1 hour and 10 minutes or until tender. When cooked, remove the chilli, thyme and orange. Add the grapes, honey, pekmez and chicken stock then cook for a further 15 minutes.

### For the mujaddara

You can make the mujaddara while the duck is in the oven. Boil the lentils in a small pan covered with plenty of water for 15 minutes or until tender but not soft. Drain and put to the side.

Heat the vegetable oil in a pan and fry the onion in two or three batches until golden brown and crispy. Place the fried onion on kitchen roll to absorb the excess oil.

Heat the olive oil in a separate pan and add the cumin seeds, lemon peel and allspice. Fry for about 1 minute until fragrant. Add the rice and stir until all the rice is coated in oil. Add the bay leaves, lentils, salt and 600ml water. Bring to the boil, cover with a tight-fitting lid and simmer on a low heat for around 15 minutes. Remove the pan from the stove and steam with the lid on for a further 5 minutes. Stir through half the onions.

### To serve

Pile the mujaddara on a plate topped with a duck leg. Pour over some of the sauce from the roasting tin and top with a handful of the remaining crispy onions. Garnish with fresh pomegranate seeds and chopped fresh flat leaf parsley.

# Good food
# STARTS HERE

Bakery, butchery, fish counter, cheese counter, food hall and a glorious café serving homemade food – Source Food Hall and Café at the heart of St Nicholas Market is a foodie paradise where, as the name suggests, everything comes down to provenance.

Although this epicurean gem has existed under the guise of Source Food Hall in St Nicholas Market since 2008, it remains one of the city's best-kept culinary secrets. When people stumble on this treasure trove of Bristol's home-grown bounty they are often amazed they hadn't known it existed.

It is run by three food enthusiasts; Liz, Ross and Joe. The three had been working there under its former identity, so when it was threatened with closure, they put their heads together and decided they were the perfect team to turn it into something extraordinary. They all felt strongly about the ethos of the business and shared a vision of making it the ultimate celebration of locally, ethically and seasonally sourced food.

Since then, they have built up close relationships with farmers and producers to gather the finest ingredients under one roof, always based on the premise of paying a fair price, selling at a fair price and never compromising on quality. The shop is managed by Joe and what is sold depends entirely on the seasons and what is available locally.

They butcher meat onsite – the Hereford cross beef is aged for at least 30 days and customers are always amazed at the difference in flavour. The fish counter teams with fish caught fresh each day by small-scale fishermen. This means they never quite know what the day's catch will contain, although one thing is for sure, if it doesn't swim in the British waters, you won't find it on the fish counter.

There is so much skill on hand to help customers put meals together. They cure their own pastrami (perfect for sandwiches), smoke their own pig's cheeks (which can be put to use in their recipe overleaf), make their own sausages, white pudding and baked beans (that's breakfast sorted!) and talented baker Liz makes all of the irresistible fresh bread, desserts and cakes each day.

All of this delicious fare is put to good use in the café where Ross, with over 20 years of experience in the kitchen, creates dishes around the daily-changing produce available. "I love the freedom of this type of cooking," he says, "where the only boundaries are set by the bounty of nature."

"We like to say that good food starts here. We source the very best so it tastes the very best." And it seems their growing group of regular customers agrees!

# Source Food Hall and Café

## PORK LOIN WITH SMOKED PIG'S CHEEK AND CLAMS

A double whammy of pork is served up with fresh clams in this delicious dish. The red pepper and broad beans create a lovely splash of colour on the plate, too.

Preparation time: 30 minutes | Cooking time: 1 hour | Serves 2.

### Ingredients

1 red pepper

60g broad beans, podded

2 new potatoes, boiled and diced

50g smoked pig's cheek, diced (made at Source)

2 pork loins (180g-200g)

130g clams

100ml white wine

25ml sherry vinegar

Oil, for frying

### Method

Preheat the oven to 200°C. Cut the red pepper in half and place on a baking tray cut-side down. Place in the oven and bake for 20-25 minutes or until the skins are wrinkled and slightly charred. Once the peppers are ready, allow to cool and then peel off the skins. Dice and put to one side.

Place the podded broad beans in a pan of boiling salted water and cook for about 3-4 minutes until the broad beans are tender. Once cooked, refresh in cold water and drain. Put in the fridge until needed.

Heat a frying pan and add some oil. Add the diced boiled new potatoes and smoked pig's cheek to the pan and fry until golden. Once cooked, keep warm in the oven.

Preheat a griddle pan or frying pan. Season the pork loin steaks with salt and pepper, rub the pork with some sunflower oil and fry for 4 minutes on each side. While the pork is cooking, preheat a saucepan. Add the clams to the saucepan with the white wine and allow the clams to steam open. Once open, add the sherry vinegar and cook to reduce, then add the peppers and broad beans to the clams.

Once the pork is cooked, place it on plates with the potato and smoked pig's cheek mix. Add the clams with the broad beans and peppers and some of the juices, and serve.

# The Spice
# OF LIFE

Famous for their enticing counter displays brimming with colourful salads, freshly prepared sandwiches, home-made tarts and stunning cakes, Spicer+Cole have opened their third shop in Gloucester Road, bringing their simple approach to fresh and healthy food to more of Bristol's foodies.

Spicer+Cole is the result of Carla and Chris Swift's dream of leaving the corporate world behind and putting all their energy into their love of good, honest food. After ditching their offices (and spending a few eye-opening years in the Andalucian hills) the duo moved to Bristol with the idea of opening their own café.

Carla had spent her career within the hotel and hospitality industries, and she and her husband were bursting with ideas for their venture. Their interest in speciality coffees, along with simple, fresh dishes, was going to form the heart and soul of the first Spicer+Cole when it opened just off Queen Square in July 2012.

The counter is a feast for all the senses. "We wanted our customers to buy with their eyes rather than trawling through long menus", explains Carla, likening the experience to feeling like a kid in an old-fashioned sweet shop. The healthy, fresh and wholesome sandwiches, salads, tortillas and soups are balanced by irresistible cakes, pastries and sweet treats. "We try to offer a range of goodies catering to all tastes and dietary requirements", enthuses Carla – their vegan banana bread with date caramel has won over many a fan.

The first shop was a huge success and the second premises in Clifton opened in September 2013; a different area but with the same love of fresh produce, honest food and supporting local independents. The third spot opened in Gloucester Road in June 2016 and again has been quickly embraced by the community.

The pair's love of cooking can be seen in every corner, from the shelves heaving with cookbooks to the window into the kitchen in the new Gloucester Road store, where diners can watch the bakers hard at work. They are also ardent supporters of using local produce, sourcing the finest ingredients from as close to home as possible – such as Extract Coffee, Waterloo Tea, Ruby & White Butchers, Abu Noor and Bertinet Bakeries.

From their famous breakfasts and brunches (which are made fresh to order and really come into their own on weekends when people can spend a lazy couple of hours indulging in brioche French toast with maple syrup and bacon accompanied by a speciality coffee) to lunch on-the-go, everything at Spicer+Cole reflects their simple aim of fresh, seasonal food – done well.

Seasonal+Tarts+Salads+Breads+

# Spicer+Cole

# RAW BEETROOT SLAW WITH SEEDS, RAISINS, HERBS AND A POMEGRANATE DRESSING

We love our 'slaws' at Spicer+Cole and you'll usually find one on the counter every day as they are so healthy and versatile. This one is a really great energy boosting salad, packed with raw veg, refreshing herbs, a zingy dressing and crunchy topping – what's not to like! We serve this in the cafe with a wedge of tortilla and some seasonal leaves, but it would work just as well with any protein like chicken or halloumi or even stuffed in a pitta with some hummus and greens for a speedy, healthy lunch on the go. If you want a completely raw salad, skip toasting the nuts – it will still taste great!

Prep time: Approx. 30 minutes | Cook time: Approx. 6 minutes | Serves 6.

## Ingredients

**For the salad:**

2 tbsp sunflower seeds

2 tbsp pumpkin seeds

50g raisins

6 medium size beetroot (different varieties work well if you can get hold of them)

3 medium size carrots

20g mint, leaves picked and chopped

20g flat leaf parsley, leaves picked and chopped

½ pomegranate

**For the dressing:**

100ml rapeseed oil (or extra virgin olive oil)

½ lemon, juice

½ orange, juice

1 tbsp pomegranate molasses

1 tsp honey

Salt and pepper, to season

## Method

Preheat the oven to 170°C. Toast the seeds in the preheated oven on a baking tray for 5-6 minutes until golden. Leave to cool.

Mix the dressing ingredients together (we like to do this by shaking vigorously in an airtight container). Soak the raisins in the dressing for a few minutes while you get on with the rest of the salad preparation.

Peel and remove the ends of the beetroot and carrots and grate them in a food processor or by hand with a grater. Mix together in a large bowl. Mix through the chopped mint and parsley (reserving some for the top).

Remove the seeds from the pomegranate by cutting it in half and tapping with a rolling pin until the seeds come out (or any method that works for you). Add to the rest of the ingredients.

Add the dressing and seasoning, and mix everything together. Serve in a bowl or platter with the reserved herbs and the toasted seeds on top.

# Spicer+Cole
# FIG, ROSEMARY AND OLIVE OIL CAKE

The inspiration for this cake originally came from an Ottolenghi apple cake recipe (which is also delicious). One of our chefs, Alex, came up with the idea when I arrived in the kitchen one day with a huge basket of fresh figs from our garden. They found their way in to many of our recipes that Autumn, but this one is a particular favourite. It's a super moist cake due to the fruit and olive oil and the flavours intensify and get even better after a day or two. Special enough to impress a loved one on their birthday, but also perfect as a Sunday afternoon treat with a refreshing cup of Earl Grey!

Prep time: Approx. 30-40 minutes | Cook time: Approx. 60-70 minutes | Serves 12.

## Ingredients

### For the cake:

120g sultanas

150g dried figs, sliced

1 sprig of rosemary

175ml fresh apple juice

3 large free-range egg whites

220g caster sugar

180ml olive oil

3 large free-range eggs

2 lemons, zest

420g plain flour

2 tsp bicarbonate of soda

¾ tsp baking powder

2½ tsp ground all-spice

½ tsp salt

½ tsp vanilla paste

Bakespray or butter, for greasing

### For the icing:

150g butter, at room temperature

150g muscovado sugar

40ml maple syrup

330g cream cheese, at room temperature

3 figs, cut into quarters

Rosemary sprigs, to decorate

## Method

### For the cake:

Grease and line a 25cm round spring-form cake tin with greaseproof paper. Preheat the oven to 170°C.

Infuse the sultanas, figs, and rosemary with the apple juice in a small saucepan, bring to the boil and simmer until the liquid has been absorbed. Remove from the heat and leave to cool (you can prepare them a few days ahead and store in the fridge). Discard the rosemary.

Whip the egg whites in a mixer fitted with the whisk attachment until stiff. Set aside. Combine the caster sugar and olive oil in a mixer on medium speed. Crack the eggs into a jug and, with the motor running on slow speed, add one egg at a time to the mixer until combined. Add the lemon zest, raisins, figs and vanilla paste, and mix until combined.

Sift the dry ingredients and then fold in to the mixture. Fold in one spoon of egg whites to loosen the mix and then gently fold in the rest until everything is combined. Pour the mixture into the cake tin. Bake in the oven for 60-70 minutes, until the skewer comes out clean. Keep checking and make sure the top doesn't brown too much (cover with foil if this happens). Leave to cool .

### For the icing:

In a mixer, cream the butter and muscovado sugar together until light and airy. Scrape down the sides of the bowl and add the maple syrup and cream cheese. Beat until well mixed and smooth.

### To assemble:

Cut the cake in half horizontally with a serrated knife and spread half the icing on the bottom half with a palette knife. Sandwich the top half of the cake on top and carefully spread the remaining icing on top. Decorate with the quartered fresh figs and rosemary sprigs.

# *Classic British* COOKING

A South Bristol favourite, The Spotted Cow is one of those rare locals where top-notch food hasn't detracted from the welcoming pub atmosphere – a real heart-of-the-community spot.

The Spotted Cow is housed in a building that has been standing in Bedminster for 200 years. It was looking a little neglected when Dave Smeaton took it over eight years ago, but he set about refurbishing the premises, restoring it and transforming it into the much-loved venue it is today.

The project was all about creating a pub that put good-quality food at the heart of things, while not neglecting that irresistible warm feeling of the community local. Good food, good drinks and good music are the things close to their heart. In essence, it had to be a pub where people could come in for a pint of real ale, to share a bottle of wine in a cosy corner and to bring the children to enjoy an afternoon in the large garden, but would also become known for serving up solid British cooking using really excellent ingredients.

Working closely with head chef Iain Webb, Dave created a dining pub that has become famous for its food. Iain is all about sourcing and building up relationships with his suppliers. He orders his fish fresh from Brixham, sources his meat from local farms and grows veggies and herbs in the roof-top garden. It brings a whole new level to the local, seasonal, sustainable and ethical food policy, having ingredients being grown just a few metres away!

His cooking has built up a huge fan base in the local area. People have to book in advance for the popular Sunday lunches – especially when it comes to the special suckling pig which is on the menu once a month and is sourced from a nearby farm. However, it's not just the locals who are coming in to eat, The Spotted Cow has now acquired such a reputation for its classic British cooking that the pub welcomes guests travelling there from miles around.

This is a community pub with honest homemade food as its backbone, and the key to The Spotted Cow's success is its broad appeal: "It's a place where we want everyone to feel welcome, whether it's families, couples or groups of friends, from the oldest to the youngest."

# BATH CHAPS, FRIED PIG'S EARS, MUSTARD MASH, CRISP CAPERS AND APPLE PURÉE

Bath chaps are a speciality of the West Country, but, given a bit of notice, any butcher should be able to prepare them for you. They consist of a boned pig's head, which is then wrapped around the tongue. If you are brave enough to attempt the butchery yourself, begin by thoroughly washing the head, making sure you get into the ears and nostrils. Then either shave the head or use a blow torch to burn the hair off. Start from under the pigs chin then work slowly around the skull, being careful not to puncture the eyes or the thin skin on the top of the skull. Prepare the chaps the day before you want to serve them, as they're much easier to use once cooked and cooled. Once cold, the chaps will keep for 5 days in the fridge. They can be eaten fried, as in this recipe, or cold, thinly sliced on toast with some cornichons.

Preparation time: 30 minutes, plus 4 hours chilling | Cooking time: 3-4 hours | Serves 4.

## Ingredients

**For the chaps and pig's ears:**

1 pig's head, boned, ears and tongue removed and set aside

5 cloves garlic, minced

1 bunch of sage, chopped

1 carrot

1 celery stick

1 bay leaf

1 white onion

Rapeseed oil, for deep-frying

Salt and pepper

**For the crisp capers:**

A handful of capers

**For the apple purée:**

1 bottle of cloudy cider

2 star anise

6 Bramley apples, peeled, cored and cubed

Honey

**For the mustard mash:**

1kg potatoes (such as Maris Piper), peeled and roughly chopped

125g unsalted butter

Wholegrain mustard

Salt and pepper

## Method

### For the chaps

Preheat the oven to 180°C. Begin with the head. Rub the minced garlic and chopped sage all over the inside, season with salt and pepper and then place the tongue in the centre. Roll the cheeks in toward the middle and tie up with butcher's string. Wrap, first in greaseproof paper, then in foil. Roast for 2½ hours, then allow to cool. Re-wrap with cling film into a big sausage shape and chill for at least 4 hours or preferably overnight.

### For the pig's ears

Bring a pan of water to the boil, add the ears, carrot, onion, celery and bay leaf, and simmer until the fat on the outside of the ears is soft; about 30 minutes. Drain, pat dry with a cloth (this is very important as the oil in the fryer will spit a lot more if they are not dry) and slice very thinly. Heat a deep fryer or a pan of oil to 180°C and fry the ears until brown and crispy. Be careful as they will pop and spit a bit, so watch your eyes. Drain on some kitchen paper and sprinkle with salt.

### For the crisp capers

In the same oil as you've just prepared the ears, drop in a handful of capers and fry until crisp. Drain on kitchen paper.

### For the apple purée

Put the cider and a couple of star anise into a pan and simmer until reduced by half, then remove the star anise and discard. Add the cubed apple and cook for 15 minutes. Use a hand blender to blitz into a purée, then add honey to taste. The purée will keep in an air tight container for a week or so.

### For the mustard mash

Cook the potatoes in a pan of salted boiling water, then drain and mash with the butter. Add some wholegrain mustard and season to taste.

### To serve

Slice the pigs head into inch-thick slices and fry in a little oil until browned on both sides. Make a puddle or swipe of apple purée on the plate, place a dollop of mash next to it, put the chaps on top of that, and scatter the capers and crispy ears over the whole lot and tuck in.

# 'Flippin' SIMPLE

When it comes to making brilliant burgers, the team at Three Brothers hold the secret to success – and it all comes down to keeping it simple with the finest ingredients the region has to offer.

Although the name might suggest a manly environment, the hectic kitchen at Three Brothers is headed up by burger wiz Gemma Mulvaney and a team that is almost entirely – yet accidentally – an all-female ensemble. And when it comes to making brilliant burgers, this is a team who have hit the nail on the head, describing their cooking as "dirty American food with a Brizzle accent".

There are probably three things that make Three Brothers stand out from the crowds – the food, the beers and the location.

Food-wise, it all starts with the ingredients. Prime Herefordshire beef is sourced from local butcher Buxton Butchers, where it is dry-aged for 28-35 days and then select cuts are combined to create the ideal mince for making the juiciest patties. It's a recipe that wasn't stumbled upon by chance – it was developed to perfection after countless recipes were tested and tasted and tested again.

Of course the perfect burger is more than just the patty itself. The soft, shiny, enriched brioche buns are made fresh each day – another recipe that has gone through endless development to ensure it is the optimum bun for holding the precious filling in place. For those wanting to mix things up, there are subs, dogs (the 100% beef frankfurters are sourced from Native Breeds, award-winning Gloucestershire charcuterie), chicken burgers, veggie options, salads and plenty of sides on the menu too.

As for the beers, executive chef Freddy Bird has a passion for local breweries that can be seen with a glance across the ten draught pumps and plethora of bottles. Around 40 beers and ciders are available at any one time and countless Bristol brewers are represented within the ever-changing selection, along with some of the most interesting craft beers from across the world.

And finally, onto that last piece of the puzzle – that glorious waterside location that is just so… well, Bristolian. Its iconic setting on a boat has the charm of outdoor seating in summer, accompanied by laid-back, chilled vibes with great music playing in the background. In the winter the great, big roaring fire is lit, so there is no need for the burgers and beers to stop flowing. Cheers to that!

# Three Brothers Burgers
## SMOKEY BRO BURGER

Three Brothers' patties are made from 100% ground 28-day aged Herefordshire beef. To this we add very light seasoning (this, I'm afraid, has to remain a secret) and it is then gently beaten in a mixer to ensure the texture has a nice bite and doesn't crumble in your mouth. Shape to your desired size but we find the 5oz patty ample. The ingredients for this burger may seem a little excessive but they need to be – that's the point of a burger! No one ever made a good burger with their health in mind!

Preparation time: 30 minutes | Cooking time: 30 minutes | Serves 4.

## Ingredients

**For the smokey bro sauce:**

2 red onions, thinly sliced

2 red peppers, deseeded and sliced

2 punnets of ripe cherry vine tomatoes, halved

A liberal squirt of good-quality BBQ sauce

A large pinch of Muscovado sugar

4 cloves garlic, finely chopped

1-2 red chillies, finely chopped

Oil, for cooking

**For the burger mayo:**

A very large spoonful of homemade or best-quality mayonnaise

2 gherkins, finely diced

1 dessertspoon capers, roughly chopped

A few sprigs of dill, finely chopped

**For the fried onions:**

2 tbsp plain flour

1 tsp fennel seeds, ground

A pinch of paprika

¼ tsp onion powder

¼ tsp garlic powder

1 red onion, thinly sliced

Oil, for deep-frying

**To build the burger:**

2 packs American or regular streaky bacon

4 beef patties, 140g/5oz each (as mentioned above)

8 slices Applewood smoked cheddar

4 best-quality brioche buns

Romaine lettuce

## Method

**For the smokey bro sauce**

Sweat the onions and peppers in oil until lightly caramelised. Next add the tomatoes, BBQ sauce and sugar and simmer over a low heat. In a separate pan fry the garlic and chillies until cooked and the edges of the garlic are just starting to turn golden. Do not let the garlic overcook; golden garlic adds a lovely richness, whereas overcooked garlic will only taste bitter and burnt. When cooked, add to the bubbling sauce, stir in and leave to simmer until you achieve a slightly 'jammy' consistency. Season to taste. (You can double up this recipe and store any leftovers in the fridge for next time.)

**For the burger mayo**

Mix all the ingredients together and set aside in the fridge.

**For the fried onions**

Mix the plain flour, fennel seeds, paprika, onion powder and garlic powder together with the sliced red onions. Heat the oil for deep-frying in a deep-fryer or heavy pan. Deep-fry the onions, then remove with a slotted spoon and set aside on kitchen paper.

**To build your burger**

Fry the bacon in a frying pan until crisp. Set aside. Cook the burgers to your liking; preferably pink so that they remain lovely and juicy! For the last minute, drop the cheese on top so that it starts to melt. Slice each bun in half, spoon on a generous dollop of the burger mayo, then a piece of romaine lettuce, then the cheese-topped patty, then the sauce, then the bacon and crispy onions. Place the bun lid on top and hold it all together with a wooden skewer. Serve and eat immediately, preferably with people who you don't mind watching you cover yourself in food!

# Striking a light for
# INDEPENDENTS

When the landmark building was saved from demolition and redeveloped into a haven for the city's creative industries, Tobacco Factory became a catalyst for regeneration in Southville – and today it is a community hub where theatre, art, design and dance are celebrated alongside healthy Mediterranean-inspired food.

The Tobacco Factory plays an important role in the Southville community due to its fascinating history. The building was derelict for years, it is today one of the few survivors from the great Imperial Tobacco site on Raleigh Road, having been rescued from the prospect of demolition by George Ferguson. A champion of independent businesses, George's vision for the building was to make it a community hub where small businesses could thrive, leading the way for regeneration of the area.

The Café Bar occupies a uniquely industrial space at the heart of the Tobacco Factory. With exposed brickwork, steel and concrete all around, it embraces and reflects the heritage of the idiosyncratic space it inhabits, while also offering its own personality into the mix thanks to the distinct Mediterranean-inspired menu.

The first of the new wave of café bars and restaurants in the area, it was one of the defining eateries around North Street, leading the way for the area to become one of the city's most thriving communities. It's a place to eat, drink and meet – where everyone is welcome.

The crowd changes throughout the day as the Café Bar welcomes people from all walks of life. This is thanks to the highly acclaimed theatre, the numerous events that are always happening and the successful Sunday Market, which has also played a huge part in bringing the Southville and Bedminster communities together.

The food takes diners right across the Mediterranean. Head chef Marcin Dzieniarz describes his menu as a journey from Spain and Morrocco to Turkey and Lebanon, via Greece and Italy. There is a relaxed approach to dining, with small plates available to share, tapas-and mezze-style, along with some stunning main dishes and desserts. And there is a great choice of drinks to accompany the food, with an excellent and constantly changing range of craft beers.

There is as much choice for food as for the type of space you want to sit in, from the vibrant café bar to the more intimate atmosphere of the Snug, and the sunny outside spaces of the terrace bar and garden. The Tobacco Factory is somewhere where no-one feels out of place.

# The Tobacco Factory

# PAN-FRIED SEA BASS WITH FENNEL SALAD AND DILL CAPER OLIVE OIL

A lovely fresh and summery dish from The Tobacco Factory, packed with flavours and textures thanks to the palate-pleasing combination of fennel, orange, pomegranate, radish and cucumber.

Preparation time: 30 minutes | Cooking time: 5 minutes | Serves 2.

## Ingredients

1 head of fennel

2 tbsp sambuca

1 pomegranate, seeds

1 orange, segmented

4 radishes, quartered

½ cucumber, finely sliced

1 tsp balsamic vinegar

A bunch of dill, finely chopped

A glug of olive oil

1 tbsp capers

4 sides of sea bass fillet

A squeeze of lemon juice, plus lemon slice to serve

Salt and pepper

## Method

Finely slice the fennel and blanch in hot water for a few seconds. Drain and add the sambuca.

Mix the pomegranate seeds, orange segments, radishes and cucumber, and add to the fennel. Add a little salt and pepper and a tsp of balsamic vinegar.

### For the dressing

mix the dill, olive oil and capers in a separate bowl.

### For the sea bass

heat a pan so it is almost smoking, then carefully add the sea bass skin-side down and fry until it starts to turn golden. Turn the fish over, cook the other side and squeeze lemon juice into the pan (add the lemon juice around the fish for a better flavour). Add salt and pepper to taste.

### To Serve

Spoon the salad onto the middle of each plate, add two sea bass fillets on top, drizzle the olive oil with capers and dill around the plate. Add lemon slice.

# Setting the STANDARD

Situated at the heart of two of Bristol's thriving high streets, The Urban Standard and North St Standard have put local produce, creative cooking, interesting drinks and a warm welcome on the menu at their brilliantly Bristolian bar and kitchens.

The Urban Standard is the product of the combined knowledge, expertise and passion of two experienced and ambitious restaurateurs. Dom Wood and Tim Moores had waited a long time for the perfect spot to become available on the thriving Gloucester Road. They had a shared vision for the stripped-back, industrial design where reclaimed 1930s tiles sit alongside iconic graffiti, but they also created irresistible warmth in the informal atmosphere.

When it comes to food and drink, executive chef Jasper Prickett explains the importance of quality: "A lot of effort is put into working with suppliers that support local, quality produce. Whether it be an independent brewery like Arbor Ales, local coffee roasters Clifton Coffee, artisan bakers Joe's Bakery, master butcher Nigel Buxton or the Real Olive Co (just to name a few), we're lucky to have such quality and diversity on our doorstep."

An experienced team in the bar and kitchen make The Urban Standard a fun place to work, and this ambience permeates the entire space, which might explain why it attracts such a diverse array of people. From groups of friends meeting for a lazy brunch or families enjoying a Sunday roast to three-course dinners and after-work cocktails, everyone feels at home here.

For Jasper, trying to sum up his diverse menu is difficult. "It tends to be crowd-pleasing, comforting food. There are some familiar and trusted favourites alongside more daring dishes influenced by various international cuisines."

Brunches range from buttermilk pancakes or "dirty beans" to homemade granola or smashed avocado on sourdough toast, as well as a perfectly executed full English. The rest of the day sees an impressively varied range of mouth-watering dishes flying out of the kitchen, from burgers, smoked pulled pork and bbq ribs to creative vegetarian options and inspired vegan dishes – not to mention freshly caught fish, huge pots of mussels, juicy steaks, hearty salads and gut-busting sandwiches.

The success led to the opening of North St Standard, in May 2015, again finding a home on an arty, independent high street. A large outdoor area draws the crowds for al fresco dining in summer and the spacious interior is ideal for large groups and work parties, as well as providing a warm welcome for families with pushchairs and curious children! It's all about a relaxed approach at North St Standard.

However, with 2016 seeing the opening of the third site in Cardiff, there is certainly no relaxing on the cards for Dom, Tim and Jasper!

# STICKY TOFFEE SUNDAE WITH SALTED CARAMEL SAUCE & PECAN BRITTLE

An indulgent sundae packed with lots of home-made goodies – salted caramel, pecan brittle and sticky date sponge. You can make the salted caramel sauce and pecan brittle while the sticky date sponge is baking, then you will just need some of your favourite vanilla ice cream to assemble your dessert! There will be some leftover sponge and brittle to save for another time.

Preparation time: 20 minutes | Cooking time: 50 minutes | Serves 8.

## Ingredients

**For the sticky date sponge:**

300g dates, chopped

500ml water

1½ tbsp bicarbonate of soda

100g unsalted butter

300g caster sugar

4 medium eggs

300g plain flour

1½ tbsp baking powder

**For the salted caramel:**

250g caster sugar

1 tbsp liquid glucose

50ml water

250ml double cream

25g unsalted butter

1 tsp sea salt

**For the pecan brittle:**

200g caster sugar

100g liquid glucose

100ml water

150g pecan nuts

A pinch of sea salt

1 tbsp unsalted butter

1 tsp bicarbonate of soda

**For the Chantilly cream:**

500ml whipping cream

1 vanilla pod

50g icing sugar

**To assemble:**

Favourite vanilla ice cream

## Method

### For the sticky date sponge

Preheat the oven to 190°C. Line a baking tray with parchment paper. Place the dates and water in a pan, bring to the boil and simmer for 5 minutes. Remove from the heat and stir in the bicarbonate of soda.

Cream the butter and sugar in a food processer until pale and fluffy. Then add the eggs, one by one, and blend until smooth. Now add the flour and baking powder and blend just enough to combine everything. Pour this batter into a mixing bowl, add the boiled date mixture and combine well. Transfer the pudding mixture into the prepared tray and bake for 45 minutes. Test by inserting a sharp knife into the centre of the pudding – the knife should come out clean. Leave to cool. Slice into bite-size pieces.

### For the salted caramel

In a heavy-based saucepan, combine the sugar, glucose and water. Warm over a low heat to slowly melt the sugar. Once the sugar has melted, turn the heat up high to boil the syrup. The syrup will begin to caramelise and turn a dark golden colour. Turn the heat down low, then add the cream, a little at a time, stirring well to combine. Add the butter and salt and stir well.

### For the pecan brittle

Line a baking tray with parchment paper. Melt the sugar, glucose and water in a pan and heat to 121°C on a sugar thermometer. Add the nuts and salt and continue to boil the syrup to 145°C. Remove from the heat, stir in the butter, followed by the bicarbonate of soda. Mix well. Pour the mixture onto the lined tray and spread thinly to cool down completely before cracking up into pieces and crushing slightly. Store in an airtight jar in a cool, dry place.

### For the Chantilly cream

Scrape the seeds from the vanilla pod and add to the cream along with the icing sugar. Whisk the cream to create fluffy, stiff peaks. Chill.

### To assemble

Warm the date sponge and salted caramel sauce and place into a suitable sundae glass along with a couple of scoops of the ice cream. Top with the Chantilly cream and pecan brittle.

# The DIRECTORY

These great businesses have supported the making of this book; please support and enjoy them.

**Ahh Toots**
4-8 Glass Arcade
St Nicholas Market
Bristol BS1 1LJ
Telephone: 07788 843960
Website: www.ahhtoots.co.uk
*An art-focussed cakery in the heart of Bristol.*

**Bambalan**
Podium Level
Colston Tower
Colston Avenue
Bristol BS1 4XE
Telephone: 0117 9221880
Website: www. bambalan.co.uk
*Fresh, healthy and exciting all day dining, an expertly crafted drinks menu, exceptional coffee and tea and unrivalled views over the city centre from our rooftop terrace.*

**Better Food**
St Werburghs Flagship Store and Café
The Proving House
Sevier Street
Bristol BS2 9LB
Telephone: 0117 9351725

**Better Food**
Clifton Food Hall and Deli
94a Whiteladies Road
Clifton
Bristol BS8 2QX
Telephone: 0117 946 6957

**Better Food**
Wapping Wharf Store and Café
1-5 Gaol Ferry Steps
Wapping Wharf
Bristol BS1 6WE
Telephone: 0117 930 7390
Website: www.betterfood.co.uk
*A trio of well-loved independent health-food stores and cafés selling organic, locally grown, ethically sourced and Fairtrade produce.*

**The Boardroom**
20 St Nicholas Street
Bristol BS1 1UB
Telephone: 0117 925 4617
Website: www.theboardroombristol.com
*The Boardroom is all about great cheeses, wines, cured meats, ciders, ales and independent beers. Get your graze on.*

**Bosh**
1 Dean St
Bristol BS3 1BG
Telephone: 07921 453294
Website: www.bosh.biz
*Bespoke caterer and private chef, supper club, provider of cake.*

**Brace & Browns**
43 Whiteladies road
Clifton
Bristol BS8 2LS
Telephone: 0117 973 7800
Website: www.braceandbrowns.co.uk
*An independent kitchen and bar boasting the hugely popular bottomless brunch, Bristol's best roast dinners and a fabulous daily small plates and mains menu.*

## Brew Coffee Company
45 Whiteladies Road
Clifton
Bristol BS8 2LS
Telephone: 0117 973 2842
Website: www.brewcoffeecompany.
co.uk
*Brunch, lunch, cake and always a bloody good brew!*

## The Bristolian
2 Picton Street
Bristol BS6 5QA
Telephone: 0117 919 2808
Website: www.thebristolian.co.uk
*Fully licenced café bistro serving delicious home-made food from breakfast to dinner.*

## The Burger Joint
Whiteladies branch
83 Whiteladies Rd
Bristol BS8 2NT
Telephone: 0117 329 0887

## The Burger Joint
Bedminster branch
240 North St
Bristol BS3 1JD
Telephone: 0117 3292790

## The Burger Joint
Fishponds branch
773 Fishponds Rd
Bristol BS16 3BS
Telephone: 0117 965 7690
Website: www.theburgerjoint.co.uk
*Probably the best burgers in Bristol, possibly the best in England!*

## Buxton Butchers
62 Bradley Avenue
Winterbourne BS32 1HS
Telephone (shop): 01454 773 213
Telephone (trade): 01275 373 339
Website: www.buxtonbutchers.co.uk
*Traditional family butchers who specialise in quality local meat, as well as supplying the finest restaurants. Famous for dry-aged steaks using Himalayan salt chambers.*

## The Canteen
Hamilton House
80 Stokes Croft
Bristol BS1 3QY
Telephone: 0117 923 2017
Website: www.canteenbristol.co.uk
*Situated in the heart of Stokes Croft, the Canteen is all about great food, free live music and a relaxed and friendly atmosphere.*

## The Clifton Sausage
7-9 Portland Street
Clifton
Bristol BS8 4JA
Telephone: 0117 973 1192
Website: www.cliftonsausage.co.uk
*The 'Sausage' specialises in traditional and classic British dishes as well as sausages, using the freshest and finest ingredients.*

## Corks of Cotham
54 Cotham Hill
Cotham
Bristol BS6 6JX
Telephone: 0117 973 1620
Website: www.corksofbristol.com

## Corks of North Street
79 North Street
Bedminster
Bristol BS3 1ES
Telephone: 0117 963 3331
Website: www.corksofbristol.com
*An independent wine and spirit merchant, we stock a hugely varied and highly sought-after range of wines, beers and spirits.*

## The Full Stop Café
within Bookbarn International
Unit 1 Hallatrow Business Park
White Cross, Wells Road
Bristol BS39 6EX
Telephone: 01761 451333
Website:
www.bookbarninternational.com/café
*Café serving delicious, original home-made food surrounded by hundreds of thousands of pre-loved books.*

## Glassboat Restaurant
Welsh Back
Bristol BS1 4SB
Telephone: 0117 332 3971
Website: www.glassboat.co.uk
*A restaurant and bar berthed in its idyllic location at Welsh Back in the heart of Bristol for 30 years.*

## Grain Barge
Mardyke Wharf
Hotwell Rd, Hotwells
Bristol BS8 4RU
Telephone: 0117 929 9347
Website: www.grainbarge.co.uk
*This historic converted barge is bursting with character, and with stunning panoramic views, it makes for a great place to soak up its harbourside location.*

## Hyde & Co.
2 The Basement
Upper Byron Place
Bristol BS8 1JY
Telephone: 0117 929 7007
Website: www.hydeand.co
*Hyde & Co is Bristol's best kept secret prohibition bar.*

## Incredible Edible Bristol
Website: www.ediblebristol.org.uk
Twitter: @EdibleBristol
Facebook: www.facebook.com/
ediblebristol
*Community food growing movement.*

## The Lazy Dog

112 Ashley Down Road

Bristol BS7 9JR

Telephone: 0117 924 4809

Website: www.thelazydogbristol.com

*A vibrant pub in the heart of the community of Ashley Down, North Bristol.*

## Lido

Oakfield Place

Clifton

Bristol BS8 2BJ

Telephone: 0117 332 3970

Website: www.lidobristol.com

*Award-winning restaurant situated on the old viewing gallery of the Clifton Pool.*

## Little Kitchen Cookery School

153 Wick Road

Brislington

Bristol BS4 4HH

Telephone: 07783 334881

*Website: www.little-kitchen.co.uk*

*Bristol's fun and affordable cookery school for adults and children.*

## The Mall Deli

14 The Mall

Clifton

Bristol BS8 4DR

Telephone: 0117 973 4440

Website: www.themalldeli.co.uk

*A traditional deli and café in the heart of Clifton Village which has been serving delicious food to our customers for 30 years.*

## Manna

2B North View

Westbury Park

Bristol BS6 7QB

Telephone: 0117 970 6276

Website: www.mannabar.co.uk

*The very best of Mediterranean-inspired cuisine.*

## The Milk Thistle

Quay Head House

Colston Avenue

Bristol BS1 1EB

Telephone: 0117 929 4429

Website: www.milkthistlebristol.com

*Hidden in one the finest historic buildings in the old city The Milk Thistle is the flirty younger sister of Bristol's hippest prohibition bar, Hyde & Co.*

## No.1 Harbourside

1 Canon's Road

Bristol BS1 5UH

Telephone: 0117 929 1100

Website: www.no1harbourside.co.uk

*Eat good food. Enjoy the finest music. Go local on Bristol's historic harbourside.*

## The Old Market Assembly

25 West Street

Old Market

Bristol BS2 0DF

Telephone: 0117 373 8199

Website: www.oldmarketassembly. co.uk

*A buzzing food and live music venue with The Wardrobe Theatre and Old Market Assembly Bakery.*

## The Olive Works

40-42 Glass Arcade

St Nicholas Street

Bristol BS1 1LJ

Telephone: 0117 909 9587

*Healthy, mouth-watering, Mediterranean-inspired salads, marinated olives and antipasti, plus our renowned Khobez flatbread wraps.*

## The Ox

Corn Street Branch

The Basement, 43 Corn Street

Bristol BS1 1HT

Telephone: 0117 922 1001

Website: www.theoxbristol.com

*Tucked away in a basement below The Commercial Rooms on Corn Street, The Ox is a bastion of simple, top-notch British fare, cooked to impeccable standards.*

## The Ox

Clifton Branch

96a Whiteladies Road, Clifton

Bristol BS8 2QX

Telephone: 0117 973 0005

Website: www.theoxclifton.com

*Purveyors of some of the city's best steaks. With a focus on great food cooked to impeccable standards, The Ox Clifton is the ultimate dining destination for all meat lovers.*

## Pata Negra

Corn Street

Old City

Bristol BS1 1YH

Telephone: 0117 9276762

Website: www.patanegrabristol.com

*A bustling, Spanish tapas and wine bar in the heart of Bristol's Old City.*

## Pinkmans

85 Park Street

Bristol BS1 5PJ

Telephone: 0117 403 2040

Website: www.pinkmans.co.uk

*Breaking with bakery tradition.*

## riverstation

The Grove

Bristol BS1 4RB

Telephone (restaurant): 0117 914 4434

Telephone (bar+kitchen): 0117 914 9463

Website: www.riverstation.co.uk

*Two floors of modern European dining on the waterfront.*

**Rosemarino**

1 York place

Clifton

Bristol BS8 1AH

Telephone: 0117 973 6677

Website: www.rosemarino.co.uk

*Open seven days a week for breakfast, brunch and lunch with aperitivo and dinner being served Tuesday – Saturday, Rosemarino is a little gem to enjoy anytime, whether it be the full Italian feast or simply for a coffee while reading the papers.*

**Salt Café**

120 St George's Road

Bristol BS1 5UJ

Telephone: 0117 329 2970

Website: www.saltcafebristol.co.uk

*Friendly cafe serving home-cooked food using locally and ethically sourced ingredients.*

**Soukitchen**

Southville

Clifton

277 North Street

Bristol BS3 1JP

Telephone: 0117 966 6880

**Soukitchen**

59 Apsley Road

Bristol BS8 2SW

Telephone: 0117 906 7690

*Authentic market food inspired by the Middle East.*

**Source Food Hall and Café**

1-3 Exchange Avenue

Saint Nicholas Market

Bristol BS1 1JW

Telephone: 0117 927 2998

Website: www.source-food.co.uk

*A unique food experience where you can buy the freshest produce from the shop and eat from a seasonally changing menu.*

**Spicer +Cole**

1 Queen Square Avenue

Bristol BS1 4JA

Telephone: 0117 922 0513

**Spicer +Cole**

9 Princess Victoria Street

Bristol BS8 4BX

Telephone: 0117 973 2485

**Spicer +Cole**

16 The Promenade

Gloucester Rd

Bristol BS7 8AE

Telephone: 0117 924 7628

Website: www.spicerandcole.co.uk

*Speciality coffee and fresh, seasonal food – done well.*

**The Spotted Cow**

139 North Street

Bedminster

Bristol BS3 1EZ

Telephone: 0117 963 4433

Website:

www.thespottedcowbristol.com

*A quality local pub with a large walled garden serving up great food, drinks and music.*

**Three Brothers Burgers**

Aboard Spyglass, Welsh Back

Bristol BS1 4SB

Telephone: 0117 927 7050

Website:

www.threebrothersburgers.co.uk

*Great burgers and an ever-changing and extensive range of craft beers and ciders.*

**Tobacco Factory**

Raleigh Rd

Bristol BS3 1TF

Telephone: 0117 902 0060

Website: www.tobaccofactory.com

*Hang out in our spacious café bar and enjoy great food, exhibitions, events and live music, delve into our weekly Sunday market or book a theatre ticket.*

**The Urban Standard**

35 Gloucester Rd

Bristol BS7 8AD

Telephone: 0117 942 4341

Website: www.theurbanstandard.co.uk

*A 'local' bar and kitchen offering quality food and drink all day and throughout the evening.*

**North St Standard**

11-13 North Street

Bristol BS3 1EN

Telephone: 0117 963 9223

Website: www.northststandard.co.uk

*An independent bar and kitchen offering quality food and drink in a laid-back atmosphere.*

# Other titles in the 'Get Stuck In' series

**The North Yorkshire Cook Book** features Andrew Pern, Visit York, Made in Malton, Black Sheep Brewery and lots more.
*978-1-910863-12-1*

**The Birmingham Cook Book** features Glynn Purnell, The Smoke Haus, Loaf Bakery, Simpsons and lots more.
*978-1-910863-10-7*

**The Oxfordshire Cook Book** features Mike North of The Nut Tree Inn, Sudbury House, Jacobs Inn, The Muddy Duck and lots more.
*978-1-910863-08-4*

**The Lancashire Cook Book** features Andrew Nutter of Nutters Restaurant, Bertram's, The Blue Mallard and lots more.
*978-1-910863-09-1*

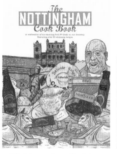

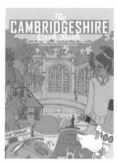

**The Sheffield Cook Book** features Baldwin's Omega, Nonna's, Ashoka, Cubana, Peppercorn and lots more.
*978-0-9928981-0-6*

**The Nottingham Cook Book** features Sat Bains with Rooms, World Service, Harts, Escabeche and lots more.
*978-0-9928981-5-1*

**The Derbyshire Cook Book** features Chatsworth Estate, Fischer's of Baslow, Thornbridge Brewery and lots more.
*978-0-9928981-7-5*

**The Cambridgeshire Cook Book** features Daniel Clifford of Midsummer House, The Pint Shop, Gog Magog Hills, Clare College and lots more.
*978-0-9928981-9-9*

**The Suffolk Cook Book** features Jimmy Doherty of Jimmy's Farm, Gressingham Duck and lots more.
*978-1-910863-02-2*

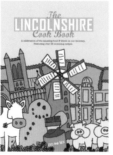

**The Manchester Cook Book** features Aiden Byrne, Simon Rogan, Harvey Nichols and lots more.
*978-1-910863-01-5*

**The Lincolnshire Cook Book** features Colin McGurran of Winteringham Fields, TV chef Rachel Green, San Pietro and lots more.
*978-1-910863-05-3*

**The Newcastle Cook Book** features David Coulson of Peace & Loaf, Bealim House, Grainger Market, Quilliam Brothers and lots more.
*978-1-910863-04-6*

**The Cheshire Cook Book** features Simon Radley of The Chester Grosvenor, The Chef's Table, Great North Pie Co., Harthill Cookery School and lots more.
*978-1-910863-07-7*

**The Leicestershire & Rutland Cook Book** features Tim Hart of Hambleton Hall, John's House, Farndon Fields, Leicester Market, Walter Smith and lots more.
*978-0-9928981-8-2*

*All books in this series are available from Waterstones, Amazon and independent bookshops.*

FIND OUT MORE ABOUT US AT WWW.MEZEPUBLISHING.CO.UK